Dr. J. McA. Taggart.

Members of the Panel.

FAMILY PLANNING
FOR ULSTER

Conference held in The Conway Hotel, Dunmurry, Co. Antrim
on Friday, 31 May, 1968
Sponsored by Ortho Pharmaceutical Limited

CHAIRMAN

DR. J. McA. TAGGART, M.B., D.P.H., B.A.O., D.P.A.
President, Northern Ireland Branch,
The Society of Medical Officers of Health

With a Foreword by
REGINALD GEORGE

BRISTOL: JOHN WRIGHT & SONS LTD.
1969

Distribution by Sole Agents:
United States of America: The Williams and Wilkins Company, Baltimore
Canada: The Macmillan Company of Canada Ltd., Toronto

Text taken from the shorthand notes of

J. F. Burns
8 Norwood Park
Belfast, BT4 8AY

SBN 7236 0229 8

PRINTED IN GREAT BRITAIN BY JOHN WRIGHT & SONS LTD. AT THE STONEBRIDGE PRESS, BRISTOL

MEMBERS OF THE PANEL

J. H. M. PINKERTON, M.D., F.R.C.O.G.
Professor of Obstetrics and Gynaecology
Queen's University, Belfast

W. EDGAR, M.B., Ch.B., D.P.H., D.C.H.
Medical Officer of Health
Northampton

MRS. THELMA GREEVES
Marriage Guidance Council of Northern Ireland

DR. G. RAMAGE, M.A., B.Sc., M.D., Ch.B., D.P.H.
County Medical Officer of Health
Staffordshire

DR. J. G. NEILL, M.B., B.Chir., M.R.C.S., L.R.C.P., D.R.C.O.G.
Chairman of the Family Planning Association
Northern Ireland

DR. A. WISEMAN, M.R.C.S., L.R.C.P., D.R.C.O.G.
Slough

CONTENTS

FOREWORD

THE National Health Service (Family Planning) Act was passed by Parliament in Westminster in July, 1967, to secure the provision of family planning services by local health authorities as part of the National Health Service. In December the Minister of Health and Social Services, Northern Ireland, supported the new Act by pointing out to all local health authorities in Northern Ireland the important contribution that family planning can bring to health and family welfare.

Acknowledged prime movers in research dedicated to the problems of fertility and its control, we at Ortho saw in these events the fruition of more than twenty-five years of endeavour. Thus inspired, we entered upon the sponsorship of a series of national conferences on family planning to develop the organization, training, and facilities to aid the effective integration of family planning services within the framework of public health authorities throughout the United Kingdom.

As with the earlier Conference on Family Planning for Britain held in London in May, 1968, we were privileged to have assembled such a distinguished and able panel to preside at the Conference on Family Planning for Ulster. These proceedings and the enthusiasm of the discussion that followed pay tribute to the outstanding contributions. We record our gratitude to the distinguished panel and to the Right Honourable Minister of Health and Social Services for his generous message in support. We believe the Ulster conference marked a significant step in bringing enlightened facilities towards the solution of this pressing problem of our time.

Ortho Pharmaceutical Limited   REGINALD GEORGE
High Wycombe, England
October, 1968

FAMILY PLANNING FOR ULSTER

MORNING SESSION

INTRODUCTION

THE CHAIRMAN

LADIES AND GENTLEMEN: It is my very pleasant duty to welcome you here as delegates to this Family Planning for Ulster Conference. Some of you have come from a very long distance; some have come from Britain to speak to us, and I would give a special welcome to people who have travelled from Britain and to those from south of the Border.

The Minister of Health and Social Services, The Rt. Hon. Mr. W. J. Morgan, J.P., M.P., had hoped to be here this morning. Unfortunately owing to another engagement he has found it impossible to come, but he sends his apologies and also a message which he has asked me to read to you. It is as follows:—

I regret that I am unable personally to attend your one-day conference because of prior commitments. Nevertheless I would ask you to accept my good wishes for the success of your gathering in Belfast today.

It was with great interest that I read about the conference which was held in London earlier this month, and I am deeply appreciative of the fact that it has been possible to organize a similar conference here in Belfast on a subject which is daily assuming an increasing prominence as an integral part of the daily life of our people, as well as our health services.

At this point it would seem appropriate for me to extend a welcome to the distinguished guests from across the water, and to express the hope that they will enjoy their brief visit to our green and pleasant land, and perhaps be sufficiently stimulated to find the time to come again some day.

Although it is only a narrow strip of water which separates us from the mainland it is on occasions an effective barrier, but this should not be taken as meaning that Northern Ireland is free from the stresses brought about by a rising population which are becoming apparent in Great Britain. On the contrary, we here are already experiencing many of the problems, both medical and social, which follow in the wake of population expansion. There is, I am sure, no doubt that these problems will become more acute if this trend continues.

Those of us who are interested in family planning can be under no illusion about the vital part it has to play as an important instrument in the prevention of ill health and the promotion of family welfare. The main problem seems to be the resistance of those who genuinely find it difficult to modify views which have become deep seated, and the task of explaining the benefits of family planning to this section of the general public is therefore not an easy one. Much of the credit for the work already done is due to the Northern Ireland Family Planning Association, and here I must pay tribute to the pioneering work done by Dr. Olive Anderson and since her retirement by Dr. Joyce Neill and her devoted band of professional and lay assistants who have continued to play an important part in the organization of Family Planning in this Province.

We are extremely pleased, Dr. Anderson, that you have been able to come here today. You are the pioneer so far as family planning in Northern Ireland is concerned, and we give you a very special welcome. When Dr. Anderson began her work on family planning it was called 'birth control' and the name of Dr. Marie Stopes was not mentioned in drawing-room company.

The Minister continues:—

The fact that we have a number of clinics flourishing is due in no small measure to their untiring efforts. Nor must we lose sight of the part played by the family doctors and hospital consultants in this important branch of preventive medicine. One great advantage of a conference such as this is that it gives those workers, and, indeed, all workers in the health services who are concerned with family planning, an opportunity to get together to discuss this difficult and controversial subject.

As is the case with every essential social service, money is a prime factor, and I need hardly tell you that this is always in short supply. That the Family Planning Association has been able to expand its activities is partly due to the financial support it has received from its many well wishers. My Ministry has also made a modest contribution to the Association's funds, and in addition circularized health authorities last December encouraging them to treat family planning as a facet of health education and to make advice and treatment on medical grounds available as necessary. It was explained that they could do this either directly or by making arrangements with the Family Planning Association. So far the response from health authorities has been reasonably satisfactory.

In conclusion I would express my grateful thanks to those who have made this conference possible. To the participants, who are very mindful of the general well-being of our people, I would express the hope that every success may attend your deliberations. And finally to those of them who have come across the Irish Sea I would offer a special word of thanks for having taken the trouble to journey to this western extremity of the kingdom.

Now, ladies and gentlemen, a brief word from me as your Chairman about the objects of this conference. In the past when society was more primitive than it is today a high fertility rate and a high birth-rate were necessary in order to ensure the survival of mankind, but this is no longer the belief in advanced society. Infant mortality and death-rate generally are so low that an average of about 3 children per family is sufficient to maintain the replacement of the population. Better social and economic conditions for our people encourage early marriage and a longer child-bearing span. These factors combined with a high fertility rate present us with a situation where some form of family planning is essential if standards of living are not to be severely impaired.

Considering the question from the point of view of the individual husband and wife, there are still many couples in our community who, on grounds of religion and conscience, would not use contraceptives in any form. One must at all times and at all costs respect the views of these couples and the ultimate decision must rest with them. But, ladies and gentlemen, the winds of change are already blowing very strongly and people of all shades of persuasion and opinion are coming more and more to realize that family planning is not only in many cases medically necessary but is in most cases socially desirable. It must be the inalienable right of every married couple, irrespective of their social class or income, to determine the number of children they will have. The quality of family life is just as important as its quantity.

Advice on marriage, contraception, and child bearing must be made readily available to all who wish to take advantage of it. All branches of the medical and allied professions—obstetricians, gynaecologists, general practitioners, midwives, health visitors, and social workers—must combine with the voluntary bodies and play a vital role in this field of health education. All these professions I have mentioned are represented here today and it is a tribute to the organizers of this Conference that they have arranged a programme with such eminent speakers whose specialities are directly concerned with family planning.

I will not stand any longer between you and your panel of speakers. You have come to hear them and I will now introduce our first speaker this morning. In any family planning programme those members of the medical profession who are particularly concerned are the obstetricians and gynaecologists. Women in maternity hospitals, in gynaecological departments, or in attendance at ante- or post-natal clinics are very often seeking advice on contraception. At this time they are most receptive to guidance and advice. All the resources of family planning must be available to them, preferably within the hospital service. Now, ladies and gentlemen, we have with us this morning an eminent obstetrician and gynaecologist, Professor J. H. M. Pinkerton. Professor Pinkerton is well known to most medical members of this audience. He is Professor of Obstetrics and Gynaecology at Queen's University, Belfast, and has travelled far afield in his profession and in his speciality. I have now great pleasure in calling on him to address the audience.

OPENING ADDRESS

J. H. M. Pinkerton

Mr. Chairman, Dr. Olive Anderson, ladies, and gentlemen: There is nothing new in the idea of family planning. As you, Sir, mentioned, in the past when world populations were small and communities agrarian, large families were desirable, especially of boys. This was partly to repair wastage due to disease, famine, war, and civil disturbances, and partly to provide pairs of hands to do the work on the land and to give mutual protection. But today the emphasis is altered and family planning, by and large, now means birth control, whether we like the phrase or not. It is increasingly recognized by parents and others that the education and rearing of children constitute an essential and most important part of reproduction. It is not enough that we should have children; it is also our continuing duty to protect, feed, and educate them. It hardly needs saying that modern education is increasingly expensive whether paid for directly or indirectly through taxation and it takes longer and longer to educate children. Nowadays, in some cases it goes on for perhaps 25 years, and few parents, therefore, can afford an indefinite number of children if they are to educate them properly. While it is my unshakeable belief that to dictate the number of children parents should have is an impertinence, at the same time I am firmly of the opinion that it is the duty of everyone who has to do with the care of women during their child-bearing years to supply them directly or indirectly with a safe and efficient means of controlling their fertility if they desire to do so. There is no doubt that the part played by the medical profession in the field of family planning as a whole has left a great deal to be desired. Indeed, we have too often been guilty of projecting personal and sometimes unreasonable moral judgements.

In the early days of family planning the dedicated women who followed Marie Stopes were subjected to ridicule and even abuse by many established male members of our profession. One rarely hears a woman disparaging contraception, and the family planning movement the world over is largely indebted to the efforts of dedicated women filled with compassion for the misfortunes of their sisters. However, in fairness to my own sex we may recall that many eminent physicians, including Lord Dawson of Penn, Lord Horder, and Lord Brain, have pleaded with eloquence and worked hard to induce doctors to accept their responsibilities in this important work. Recently, the President of the College of Obstetricians and Gynaecologists, Sir John Peel, pointed out that 'A country that appears to want abortion free and easy, and contraception expensive and difficult has its priorities curiously awry'. This remark is all the more relevant when we remember something that was not clearly understood until relatively recently—namely, that criminal abortion is not something that occurs to unmarried and promiscuous girls but rather to respectable but desperate married women, amongst whom it accounts for approximately one-quarter of maternal deaths in England and Wales year by year. A clause in the new Abortion Law in the United Kingdom stipulates that this law shall not apply to Northern Ireland. I am sure that all of us on whom the burden of applying the law would fall are heartily glad that it does not. Nevertheless—and the Minister touched on this point in his message to us—the pressures that have produced the recent change across the Irish Sea exist here also and are gradually building up. If we are to avoid the unhappy consequences of a mounting demand by a public, incompletely and sometimes erroneously informed, for termination of unwanted pregnancies we must speedily set our own house in order and make easily available to all who desire them safe and reliable methods of contraception.

But the medical profession is not the only social group guilty of lack of enthusiasm for family planning. Many religious and political leaders are also at fault. Peculiarities in present attitudes often have their roots deeply embedded in the past and it is of interest to consider in this light the apathy and even antipathy still shown towards family planning in our community today. This is not confined to any one stratum of society but is to be found lurking amongst all social and religious groups.

As with many other anomalous attitudes, e.g., the refusal to allow children to play in public parks on Sundays, misinterpretation of the Christian ethic is mainly to blame for the puritanical attitude that sex is a major evil. In the past the Christian Church had taken the patristic view that any form of contraception was a sin against Nature. Saint Augustine, early in the fifth century, wrote: 'Whosoever uses copulation for the pleasure that is in it, not referring the intention to the end intended by Nature, acts against Nature.' Between the sixth and eleventh centuries there appeared at intervals a species of textbook in which the various sins and their prescribed punishments were arranged by subject matter for the guidance of parish priests. In these 'penitentials', as they were called, contraception was equated with homicide and attracted equally heavy punishments. These usually involved very prolonged periods of fasting, sometimes lasting as long as 15 years. Gradually, however, a system of commuting fasts to shorter periods of prayer was introduced, I am glad to say, in Ireland, since it was also here that many of the penitentials were first written. Eventually this more lenient attitude spread over Europe reflecting the more reasonable attitude of the parish priests who had to apply these Canon laws in practice. Standard mitigations were also established, as, for instance, for the poor. Thus it was held that in deciding punishment for contraception it 'makes a big difference whether she is a poor woman [*pauperina*] acting on account of the difficulty of feeding her children, or whether she acted to conceal fornication'.

Although Saint Thomas Aquinas in the thirteenth century still declared that 'the end which Nature intends in copulation is offspring to be procreated and educated', gradually over the ensuing centuries this stern Augustinian dictum was watered down and even in the Roman Catholic Church the use of the so-called 'safe period' was grudgingly approved by 1880, guardedly popularized between 1930 and 1950, and eventually fully sanctioned by Pope Pius XII in 1951. The substantial split between sexual intercourse and procreation already achieved by the gradual rejection of Augustinian theory was thus confirmed in practice. More emphasis was now placed on the Christian education of children and less on their procreation.

The parallel change in the Anglican Communion is clearly outlined in the Report of the 1958 Lambeth Conference Committee on the Family in Contemporary Society, where it is concluded that the traditional emphasis on the importance of procreation of children in marriage has been at the expense of that placed upon the mutual society, help, and comfort that husband and wife ought to have, to one of the other. Here, indeed, was a revolution in the Anglican understanding of marriage, so that child bearing is now regarded as only one, and not even necessarily the primary, purpose of marriage. Emphasis is increasingly placed upon the unique relational and unifying character of marriage as it affects the couple concerned.

It would perhaps have seemed likely that the Free Churches would have had less far to go to reach this position, but there is evidence that a lingering puritanism still regards sexual behaviour, even in marriage, as something less than good and only entirely acceptable if child bearing is the sole aim. Nevertheless, it is true in general that the Anglican and non-episcopal Churches are united today in proclaiming that the relational is not to be subordinated to the procreational in marriage, and, I think, that the Roman and Orthodox Churches are not far behind. It may be said, therefore, that family planning and contraception are now recognized by all Christian people as desirable both for the individual and the community.

This change in the general attitude towards sexual behaviour, and to contraception in particular, is reflected in a recent important Act of Parliament at Westminster. In 1967 the National Health Service Family Planning Act was placed on the Statute Book and on 4 Dec. in the same year our own Ministry of Health and Social Services sent a circular to the Secretary of each health authority. This important and most welcome document pointed out that in the view of the Ministry of Health and Social Services family planning can make an important contribution to the prevention of ill health and to family welfare. It went on to say that the power to provide health education and preventive services for such purposes rests on local authorities, and that general medical practitioners are also concerned with family planning advice, and may provide it as part of the general medical care of their patients. In practice, the circular continues, authorities may find it convenient to make arrangements with the Northern Ireland Family Planning Association to provide appropriate advice and treatment. Where health authorities decided to develop family planning services in collaboration with the Association, the Ministry will accordingly expect them to contribute towards the costs incurred by the Association in establishing clinics in their areas. Such contributions will rank for grant aid in the normal way. Further, in order to help the Association to build up an adequate working fund the Ministry is prepared to contribute to the Association one pound for each pound contributed by way of subscriptions and donations from other sources, including health authorities, over a 3-year period.

So far so good, but how disappointing as one continues reading to find that this contribution from the Ministry is subject to a maximum of £2500, when one compares this with the large sums of money at present being spent, no doubt rightly, on cardiac ambulances and the care of hopelessly premature infants and the mentally handicapped. A sum of £800 a year seems an unconscionably small fraction of a Ministry of Health expenditure of £110,000,000. Nevertheless, we are grateful for ministerial mercies, however small, and at least family planning has at last received official recognition.

The Ministry of Health, however, cannot itself do the actual work. Its main function is to provide moral and financial support. To whom shall it delegate the day-to-day running of this service? Rightly or wrongly, we have a trifid maternity service and while it lasts I believe that all three branches should be involved in family planning. Everyone who is concerned with reproduction should be concerned with contraception. There is a part to play for the hospitals, the public health authorities, and the family doctor. With regard to the hospitals I believe that family planning advice should be available in all obstetric and gynaecological units, and a clinic where the various techniques can be applied should be part of every major hospital out-patient department.

These will need staff to run them. At the present moment in the Royal Maternity Hospital we are fortunate in having a contraceptive service which is increasing by leaps and bounds and requires at present at least three doctor sessions a week. But the Northern Ireland Hospitals Authority only pays for one of these; another is paid for out of research funds and the third is not paid for at all. In such circumstances the service would not exist for long were it not for its value to my department for teaching and research purposes and especially were it not for the dedication and self-sacrifice of Dr. Joyce Neill who runs it. Dedication and self-sacrifice are admirable but rare qualities and they are becoming rarer in State-run concerns. If we expect to run our hospital family planning clinics on them we will have to wait a long time. The hospital authorities will have to realize the importance of this work and budget accordingly. Vast sums are not involved and the results, I believe, are in the long run far more important than the temporary salvage of the incurable.

The response by public health authorities to the Ministry circular has inevitably varied throughout the Province. I am glad to say that in many cases an excellent beginning has been made. In particular the City of Belfast has got off to a flying start and will undoubtedly develop its family planning clinics rapidly due to the energy and enlightened attitude of our Chairman, Dr. Taggart. I wish I could say the same of all our towns and cities, but inevitably there are over-conservative attitudes and vested interests to be overcome. Overcome they will be if not by our efforts then by public opinion, which is fast awakening even here in the Ulster country-side to the importance of family planning and to the rights of all our citizens in this respect.

And what of the family doctor? It seems likely that in future group practice will be the rule rather than the exception even amongst us rugged Ulster individuals. One partner in each group might well include within his sphere of special interest medical, or as the Americans say, office gynaecology. Facilities are increasingly available for training in this field which, I believe, is more rewarding and more suitable for the family doctor than obstetrics. Released from the responsibilities and frustrations of domiciliary midwifery, he could then concentrate, with great benefit to his patients, and satisfaction to himself, on the prophylaxis and early diagnosis of cancer of the breast and pelvic organs and the treatment of gynaecological complaints, minor only from a surgical point of view. The experience thus gained would make him a most suitable person to select and apply the increasingly complex techniques of contraception available today.

Mr. Chairman, the time is ripe for, and the Government and people are beginning to recognize the great importance of, family planning in the modern world. It behoves all of us doctors concerned with the well-being of womankind, whether we work in general practice, in public health, or in hospitals, to organize ourselves to play our part in this most important task. To this end conferences like today's contribute greatly and I am sure we are all most grateful to Mr. Reginald George and Ortho Pharmaceuticals for helping to make it possible.

THE CHAIRMAN: Thank you, Professor Pinkerton, for a most stimulating opening paper. Professor Pinkerton mentioned the responsibility of the local health authorities. We have two eminent medical officers of health from Britain with us today, Dr. W. Edgar and Dr. G. Ramage. Dr. Edgar is the Medical Officer of Health for Northampton. He was formerly in the City of Bradford as Deputy Medical Officer of Health, and in thinking of the Bradford situation I realize that he must have seen a lot of the great social problems arising from that area's large influx of immigrants. Family planning must have been very much in his mind when he saw conditions there. Dr. Edgar has got well away with family planning in his area and I would now ask him to tell us something about his point of view on the subject.

FAMILY PLANNING AS A PUBLIC HEALTH SERVICE

W. Edgar

I should first of all like to say how delighted I was to receive the kind invitation to take part in this morning's Conference. I think I had better tell you at the start that some 20 years ago my wife and I spent our honeymoon in this delightful country, although, as I recall, I do not think the subject of family planning concerned us.

As Professor Pinkerton has mentioned, the National Health Service Family Planning Act of 1967 received Royal Assent last year. It enables local health authorities in England and Wales to provide family planning for any person on social grounds and not, as formerly, exclusively on medical grounds. The Act has, however, two shortcomings. The first is that at present it is permissive and not mandatory; and, secondly, it is directed exclusively at local health authorities. I feel that family planning is an integral part of the health service provided by hospitals, local authorities, and general practitioners.

Before presenting my case for family planning as a public health service I should like to mention very briefly the present position in relation to family planning. In 1961 a family planning survey showed that approximately 70 per cent of married couples in Great Britain were using some method of birth control—predominantly male. At first sight this might appear a not too unsatisfactory situation, but the survey showed that many methods used were unreliable and even unsatisfactory and not based on any sound professional advice.

Whilst it is clear, therefore, that family planning is already widely practised in England and Wales, there are two important provisos. The first of these is that this is not so among the lower social groups in which delay in practising birth control and failure to adopt it at all are more common. For example, in the Registrar-General's classes I and II 80 per cent of those married within the preceding 10 years practised some form of birth control, but in the social classes IV and V fewer than 60 per cent practised it. Therefore those with large families might appear to be most in need of family planning advice. The second point was that the methods that were predominantly used were least satisfactory from the woman's point of view, both with regard to unreliability of the method and also the unreliability of the husband.

I think it is very significant that the new methods of birth control—the cap, the pill, and the intra-uterine device—are female methods, where the prime responsibility falls upon the woman rather than upon the husband. The freedom from uncertainty and continual anxiety in the mind of the woman accompanying the use of these methods requires no great stretch of imagination, even on the part of the male. Is not one of the most fundamental of all women's rights the right to avoid an unwanted preg-nancy? It is also significant that these newer methods of contraception, which are more effective and reliable, are medical methods, and increas-ingly, therefore, doctors and nurses in local authorities, in hospitals, and in general practice will become more involved with the subject of family planning as women increasingly demand what they have been denied far too long.

As the Chairman mentioned, medical science has been responsible for lowering death-rates, during birth and infancy in particular but to some extent throughout life. The hazards of massive population destruction by famine or by major diseases like small-pox and malaria are much less than they were. In consequence birth-rates and populations have increased dramatically in recent years. In developing countries, *population control* is the principal motivating force towards a better control of high birth-rates. In the more sophisticated countries *family planning* is motivated by the desire to improve the standards of living for families and their children. Unfortunately, as I have already mentioned, this is least in evidence for those families in the low-income groups in which high parity is more common. There are signs at last that the medical profession, having con-tributed so much to the creation of this problem, is now addressing itself to solving it.

So far the story of family planning in this country is one of prolonged effort on the part of a dedicated voluntary service. The local authority, the family doctor, and the hospital services have been slow to accept responsibility in this field, partly from apathy, partly from complete absence of training in this subject, and, until recently, lack of adequate statutory authority because, prior to the Family Planning Act, the only acceptable grounds were where pregnancy was considered detrimental to the health of the expectant mother.

The main reason why family planning is the concern of doctors is the profound effect on health and welfare of child bearing. The timing, spacing, and even limitation of births obviously influence the health of the mother, and her relief from constant anxiety and uncertainty must surely have a beneficial effect not only on herself but on her family.

It might be thought that population control was irrelevant in our country, yet the Government has well-established plans for more new towns and expansion of existing towns in England and Wales to cope with the present overspill problem. Further, the Registrar-General estimates that by the year 2001 the population in England and Wales will have increased from $48\frac{1}{2}$ million to nearly 65 million, an increase of $16\frac{1}{2}$ million people in England and Wales in the next 33 years. Another illustration of this is to be found in my own town of Northampton, which is about to be involved in one of these expansion schemes which, within 15 years, might well double the population of Northampton from 120,000 to a quarter of a million people.

No doubt you will be interested in the figures for Northern Ireland. Here let me say that I sent to your Chief Medical Officer a number of queries and I received replies almost by return of post. Had I written to my colleagues in the Ministry of Health in England I might still be awaiting their replies. I understand that the present population here in Northern Ireland is 1,491,000 and the Registrar-General's estimate for the year 2001 is no less than 2,290,000, an increase of over 601,000 (40 per cent) in this Province in the next 30 years!

Professor Lafitte, in a private communication to me, says this: 'Unless at least two-thirds of all married couples confine themselves to having only two or three children and allowing for the inevitable group who will have no children or only one—then Britain will have an insuperable problem of population control.'

Population control is concerned with the health and welfare of the community, whilst family planning, the subject of this Conference, is concerned with the health and welfare of the individual family and its members. Although we are more concerned with the latter today we cannot ignore the implications of population growth in this country, by which I mean not only England and Wales but Northern Ireland as well.

In the practice of social medicine the medical officer of health is concerned with those influences, environmental and social, which affect the health of the community. As a community physician, he is more aware than most of those indices—illegitimacy, illegal abortion, divorce, broken homes, unwanted children, problem families, and so on—which are manifestations of individual family and social ill health. One has only to consider briefly some of the effects of lack of family planning to appreciate the challenge facing us.

Very briefly I should like to look at three such examples. First of all there is abortion. Estimates of illegal abortion in this country have varied between sixty and one hundred thousand, a terrible toll of potential life to say nothing of the possibility of the permanent ill health to many of the mothers. A large number of mothers who seek to have abortion procured are mothers of large families who cannot face the thought of bearing and bringing up yet another child. Unfortunately the lower social classes have been at a distinct disadvantage, and whilst the Abortion Act may assist these women in that it enables the health of the family to be taken into account as well as that of the mother herself, it is dealing with the event after it has occurred. Furthermore, the legalization of abortion in Japan, Hungary, Czecho-Slovakia, and Sweden has not led to any great diminution in criminal abortions in these countries. There is a maxim in public health—'If preventable, why not prevent it?' Family planning is a truly preventive service and if readily available in an acceptable manner would do more to assist this problem than any other.

Your Chief Medical Officer informs me that the problem in this Province is probably less than it appears to be in England and Wales, but 3 women died in Northern Ireland in the past 4 years as a result of criminal abortion.

The other day I noted a headline in a newspaper, 'Abolish Abortion by Contraception'. I was more startled to read who the speaker was: none other than the Bishop of Woolwich. The Bishop said that it was impossible to make people moral by the threat of consequences. To use the lives of unwanted babies as the threat seemed to him a curious buttress for morality. 'Certainly I could never wish to keep my daughters moral by such means. I have no desire to encourage them in sexual intercourse outside marriage, but if that were their choice I should be grateful for them to go to an advice clinic.'

The second index I should like to look at is illegitimacy. Over 60,000 illegitimate babies are born in England and Wales every year. There are also 600,000 illegitimate children under school-leaving age. Such figures cover a wide spectrum of human situations. The basic problem is usually seen as the moral one of conception out of wedlock, and the punitive attitude of society, which insists that the 'wages of sin is birth' unless the situation is saved by marriage, rebounds cruelly on the innocent, unwanted child. Whilst the child may be legitimized by marriage of the parents either before or after birth and the social problems considerably modified, it is well known that premarital pregnancy is not the best foundation for a happy and successful marriage, particularly amongst young people, amongst whom the divorce rate is extremely high in England and Wales. One in three teenage brides are pregnant at the time of the wedding. In Northern Ireland the Chief Medical Officer informs me there were 1025 illegitimate children in 1960.

The third index I want to touch on is the rather wider problem of unwanted children. During 1967 over 53,000 children were received into care. I am not suggesting that all these were unwanted children, but of that number nearly 20,000 could be regarded as unwanted or lacking adequate parental care amounting to rejection. In round figures, I have obtained the following information from the most recent report of the Home Office: Deserted by mother, 5000; fit person order, 5000; illegitimate, 3000; family homeless, 2500; unsatisfactory home conditions, 1500; parent in prison, 1000; abandoned, 600. Such figures, whilst staggering in themselves, cannot convey the damage to the emotional development and mental health of many of these children deprived of the birthright of every child—to be wanted and to enjoy a happy home life. On the other hand, the lot of the unmarried mother, involving the care of her illegitimate child, is a very hard one and my view is that the dice are loaded heavily against her. Her chances of succeeding are remote in the extreme. Again, if preventable, why not prevent it?

Valid and acceptable though these arguments may be, it is rather on the grounds of making a positive contribution to the health of the mother and her family that the case for family planning as a public health service is based.

Although it is probably true that a number of mothers have large families because they like children, many women do so not out of choice but because of apathy, lack of knowledge, or unwillingness to attend existing clinics. As long ago as 1949 the Royal Commission on Population noted two interesting points. The first was that in nearly every income range parents with a family of several young children were at a disadvantage. Even where the income was high enough to rule out any question of actual want, the support of a fair-sized family often entailed very large sacrifices of comfort and amenity.

The second point was the heavy burden carried by the working mother with several children. Far too often, too frequent and too many children are reflected in increasing stress and strain within the family, deterioration in health and efficiency of the mother, and failure to meet the emotional needs of the young children. Family planning should be regarded as a positive contribution to the health and welfare of the mother and her family, and enable her to have the number of children which she and her husband choose without endangering her health and that of the children.

More than any other groups doctors and nurses and social workers see the unfortunate effects of too frequent and too many children, not only on the health of the mother but on the life of the family—increasing inability to cope, disorganization, and, in the case of some social problem families, squalor and failure to meet the basic needs of the children. Nothing is more certain than that the children in their turn will perpetuate this situation when their time comes.

Every bit of evidence suggests that these women are bearing children involuntarily and that their high fertility is based on lack of motivation, lack of information, and lack of advice and help. Surely it is negligent to deplore this state and then fail to protect an already large family from the demands of yet another unwanted member. Too many women at the present time leave maternity hospital without being asked what is probably the most important question of all: What about the next baby?

I was staggered to read in an editorial of the *British Medical Journal* of 4 May of this year these words: 'There is little point in offering contraception advice to women who are pregnant.' What absolute rubbish!

Quite apart from these important groups there is a general need to make advice on family planning available to those who, wisely, want to achieve the desire of planned parenthood, even though no risk to health is involved. There is a general need to make advice on family planning available to those who want it. As our own Minister said in his message to the

Professor J. H. M. Pinkerton.

Mrs. Thelma Greeves.

The audience.

Dr. A. Wiseman.

Dr. W. Edgar.

Dr. G. Ramage.

Conference in London: 'Family planning is not a restriction on human life but an enrichment.'

I am sure, Mr. Chairman, that I have said enough to convince all open-minded members of the audience of the case for family planning. It remains for me to suggest briefly what might be done, since it may well be that many local authorities are anxious to extend their services but financial restrictions, as well as the problem of recruiting and training suitable staff, must be a limiting factor for some time to come.

The first point I wish to emphasize is the need for education, the provision of in-service training for staff at all levels. Secondly, ample opportunity for mothers, when they are at the stage of receptiveness, to discuss the advantages for themselves and for their family of planned parenthood. Thirdly, and again in the field of education, instructing the pupils in secondary modern schools and technical colleges in the underlying virtues of self-control as well as birth control. To provide family planning advice and services, which should be readily available and acceptable to women, requires not only the closest co-operation between local authorities, general practitioners, hospital and voluntary agencies, but a fairly determined effort on the part of those responsible. I would not wish you to go away with the idea that in talking about family planning and clinics I am merely talking about pill-dispensing depots. It has a much wider concept than that.

Amongst members of our own profession and amongst members of the public we will find apathy, unwillingness, and lack of interest and we have to accept this as a fresh challenge. In England and Wales we now have the means at our disposal of making family planning readily available to all who need it. The time has come to provide these services. Achieving this goal—effective family planning available for all and equality of opportunity to obtain its means—will not necessarily eliminate the fertility differential between the low and middle social classes; nor will it eliminate all illegitimate births and early teenage pregnancies; but it can prevent many of the thousands of unwanted and unplanned babies born each year amongst all social and economic groups and some of the many thousands of illegal abortions.

Family planning should, however, be regarded primarily as a means whereby responsible parents can ensure that children arrive when they are wanted. Injury to health, not only from the effects of repeated pregnancies but from the demands from an ever-increasing number of children, is charactertistic of a small but important group of mothers in the lower social groups, whose difficulties are frequently aggravated by low income, social incompetence, and so forth. To these mothers family planning has much to offer, both as a means of preserving their own health and of safeguarding the development and well-being of their children. Family planning can make a positive contribution to happy home life and as such should form an integral and important part of our health services.

3

An extension of the present family planning services is seen not only as a means of safeguarding the health of mothers and of building loving and stable families, but as a means of tackling some of the grave social problems of our time. Not only is family planning a preventive health service; it is an integral part of any maternity service and deserves a higher priority than it has yet received. When health, as defined by the World Health Organization, is considered as complete physical, mental, and social well-being, and not merely the absence of disease, then surely it is indisputable that the spacing of pregnancies and the attendant benefits contribute not only to the physical and mental health of the mother but also to the well-being of the family as a whole. The alternatives of unwanted pregnancies, illegal abortions, unwanted children, deserted infants, and socially disturbed families is surely too high a price to pay. There is in my view no better group to assume the responsibility with regard to the provision of responsible planned parenthood than the medical profession itself.

Behind this modest Family Planning Act of last year lies enormous scope, not only for safeguarding the health of the mother and the building of a stable and happy family life, but also for tackling many of the grave social problems of our time. The best preventive for social ills in our country is a stable and loving home life for our children who arrive by choice and not by chance. The initiative to provide this service lies with us.

THE CHAIRMAN: Dr. Edgar has given us a tremendous amount of material for our study and I should like to thank him most sincerely for his contribution. This question of the number of brides under the age of 20 who go to the altar already expectant mothers created some publicity when it was mentioned in London some weeks ago, and I should like to have had the Northern Ireland statistics to see whether our own people are a bit more moral and less promiscuous than the teenagers in Britain. Unfortunately our Registrar-General's statistics are not framed in such a way that it is possible to extract this information. Perhaps at some later time it might be possible to get those figures. It is a very startling figure and a terrible revelation of the shotgun type of marriage which is common in this particular type of problem.

Ladies and gentlemen, we now come to the marriage guidance side of this problem. Society contains a mixture of statutory and voluntary bodies whose prime function is to help the family, co-operating with each other to a greater or lesser degree, sometimes unfortunately to a lesser degree. This is Human Rights Year and the Declaration of Human Rights says that the family is a natural and fundamental group, uniting society, and the family is entitled to the protection of society and the State. The stability of marriage and family life is very much the concern of those engaged in marriage guidance.

Our next speaker, Mrs. Thelma Greeves, is a member of the Marriage Guidance Council of Northern Ireland. She has been a Marriage Guidance

Counsellor since 1957, and has been engaged in the education of young people in personal relationships in schools, in industry, and in youth clubs. She has been a member of the Northern Ireland Marriage Guidance Council since 1960, and was the first counsellor to hold discussion groups in Borstal institutions. Because of her successful work she has quite recently been appointed by the Minister of Home Affairs to be the first woman member of the Visiting Committee of the Northern Ireland Committee of Borstal Institutions. I shall now ask Mrs. Greeves to address us.

MARRIAGE GUIDANCE AND FAMILY PLANNING

Thelma Greeves

First of all I should like to thank Ortho Pharmaceuticals for inviting a Marriage Guidance Counsellor to speak to you this morning. I feel that the more people who know about the Marriage Guidance Council the more useful we will be to the community in which we live.

One of the principles of the National Marriage Guidance Council is that children are the natural fulfilment of marriage and enrich the relationship between husband and wife, but nevertheless scientific contraception when used according to conscience within marriage can contribute to the health and happiness of the whole family.

May I at the outset make it crystal clear that the Marriage Counsellor does not give advice? This idea, possibly because of our name, has grown up and has been nurtured by the public who are unaware of our function. The fact is, the counsellor has a unique contribution to make. If he can give up trying to produce the answer out of a hat, give up trying to be an advice giver, give up trying to be an expert, give up trying to hurry, give up wanting to change people, lecture them, or impose his own standards on them, or run their lives for them—if the counsellor can really give up all these favourite ways of treating unhappy people, then something very important indeed may happen. When emotions of any kind have so entered into a situation that it can no longer be dealt with sensibly, then that is the time for the experience called 'counselling'.

The most important part of a counsellor's work has to do with the personal emotional relationship between the partners to the marriage, their feelings about one another and about the marriage, their convictions and prejudices, their qualities of personality, of character, and of temperament; the meanings they attach to the events of their married life and particularly to changes of circumstance or changes in their partner.

Counsellors are most carefully selected and trained before they start counselling. One is sometimes surprised at how much the National Marriage Guidance Council expects from someone who is a voluntary worker. I make no excuse for the rigorous selection and training, and as a counsellor and selector of many years' standing I realize only too well how necessary this selection and training procedure is. The difficulty is that counsellors are not dealing with problems but with people. More important still, they are nearly always dealing with people whose emotions are aroused and often confused.

It is very unusual for someone to come to a counsellor and tell his troubles in a cool, matter-of-fact way. Usually he comes as a last resort, having tried to solve the difficulties himself. Often he has sought help and advice from many other sources, relatives, friends, neighbours, doctors, clergy, or advice columns in magazines, all of whom are liable to pass him on to us. I was interested at the weekend to read in the Colour Supplement of *The Observer* an article on the 'aunties' in women's magazines. One of the 'aunties', I think it is the one in *Woman's Own*, says she sends 75 per cent of the women who write to her along to the local Marriage Guidance Council. Needless to say, nothing like that number come.

As far as family planning is concerned, a counsellor has a loyalty to both husband and wife in the marriage. One does not encourage a wife or a husband to use contraceptives without the full knowledge of the other partner. I sometimes wonder when a client goes to a family planning clinic for help, if this aspect is fully considered. This is something that we feel should be talked about, discussed, and agreed upon. Respect and trust between a married couple are every bit as important as love. It would not be correct to say that the small planned family is necessarily any happier than the large family. There are a great deal more important factors to be considered, and the happiness of a family does not bear any relation to its size. However, the fact that parents can choose to plan and limit their families makes for a great deal more pleasure and security within the home.

The sexual side of marriage is not any more important than the personal or parental relationship. It only becomes important if something is wrong with it. How often do men complain that their wives are cold and frigid? How often do women grouse about the selfishness of their husbands and the fact that they appear to be oversexed? In so many of these cases the truth is the fear, and sometimes the terror, of another unwanted pregnancy. Sexual intercourse within the marriage is the ultimate way of showing one's love and respect for one's partner. If a wife becomes neurotic and nervous how can she possibly relax and give of herself? As Dr. Eustace Chesser says in his book *Woman and Love*: 'Sometimes the obstacle to sexual satisfaction is merely that an unsuitable method of birth control is used. The unfortunate couple were previously inhibited by fear of pregnancy. To overcome this they use a contraceptive, but the expected gain does not materialise.'

We find that a request for help with contraceptives is very often the 'presenting problem', and we try to deal with the underlying uncertainties and fears. We send our clients to the Family Planning Association when they ask for help with contraceptive difficulties. We appreciate it if our client can be encouraged by the Family Planning Association to continue with counselling. I am sure you will agree that the practical solution of a suitable contraceptive does not by any means always resolve the emotional problem within the marriage.

When I meet cases like this it is a great relief to know that they can be helped by the Family Planning Association in Belfast. I have a great admiration for Dr. Olive Anderson, Dr. Joyce Neill, and their colleagues. They have fought an uphill battle in Ulster and they deserve the very greatest credit. I know of a number of marriages they have helped by their consideration, their sensitivity, and their understanding, and I wish them every success in the future. The Family Planning Association in Ulster has always helped and co-operated with the Northern Ireland Marriage Guidance Council, and on behalf of our counsellors I should like publicly to say, 'Thank you'.

In the 1930's when the Family Planning Association was formed 'contraception' was a dirty word. It was the kind of thing one did not discuss. In the forties many couples were practising family planning but it was still not brought out into the open. Today, in the late sixties, the whole climate of public opinion has changed. Thanks to frank discussion on radio and television the public can discuss their attitude and I understand that about 75 per cent of all couples who were married during the past 10 years are using some form of birth control.

In the early years of marriage a young couple need time to mature and to adjust to each other. I have always considered that the first year of marriage is the most difficult and there has been a steady increase in the number of young married couples coming to us for help. This does not mean that there are necessarily more difficulties in early marriage than ever before. It does mean (1) that young people expect more from marriage than they did 20 years ago. Young women are now men's equals in almost every profession and this has undoubtedly put a new slant on the way a woman looks at marriage. Young people today want their marriages to succeed and are prepared to work at making them succeed. (2) The Marriage Guidance Council has been accepted as a confidential service that is prepared to help those in marriage difficulties and, indeed, in preparation for marriage.

The arrival of a child in early marriage when the romantic and emotional interests of the parents are concentrated on each other could lead to strain between the parents or neglect of the child. The child interferes with the pleasure and the social life of the couple and often leads to the father continuing with his adolescent pattern of social life outside the home, leaving his frustrated wife and unwanted child behind. This is one of the big problems of early marriage today: the young wife torn between her child and her immature young husband, who still wants to think he is 'one of the boys'. There is no doubt that this situation is more apparent if the young people have had to get married.

One finds that the young couple who have become engaged, have planned where they are to live, and have discussed fully if the wife is continuing to work will undoubtedly have also decided which form of contraceptive they intend to use. Not only will they have decided, but the girl will have consulted her doctor and have started her course at least two or three months before the wedding day. But these are the mature young people and in my experience the most difficult task in life is to help immature people to mature. In the Marriage Guidance Council we find again and again that our clients are immature. I will admit that they may be 20 years of age or that they may be 55 years of age, but they are still immature in their attitudes and outlooks; perhaps the older they are the more difficult it is to help them.

The Abortion Act is now law in England and Wales and one waits with interest to see if it will be introduced into Northern Ireland. In a community such as ours it would certainly cause great controversy. Nevertheless, the new Act looks like a communal affirmation that children should be born only when their parents want them. The illegal abortion rate has been running at about 80,000 a year and it has been estimated that the demand for abortions is about 200,000 a year. Easier abortion is the less desirable method of preventing unwanted births, but contraceptive advice services are not adequate enough.

Please do not forget the hundreds of married couples who have suffered great unhappiness because they have been unable to have a child of their own. In providing family planning facilities it is hoped that you will continue to help this small minority of people who want to expand, rather than limit, the size of their family. Consultants are always most helpful with this particular problem and make appointments to see our clients at a fertility clinic. We are indeed fortunate in our panel of medical and psychiatric consultants who are never too busy to listen to a particular difficulty.

I should now like to draw your attention to the work done by counsellors in education, Most people think our work is confined to marriage counselling but a very great deal of our time is spent in working with young people. Young people grow up today in conditions both of freedom and uncertainty. This is a challenge to all who are concerned with their welfare. We have to meet the personal as well as the vocational needs of the young if we are to help them to develop those attitudes and values which make them responsible citizens in a changing world. We run group discussions in grammar schools, secondary schools, training colleges, youth clubs, with apprentices in industry and in the Borstal institution at Woburn House, Millisle.

These courses are on personal relationships. We help young people to understand themselves better and to understand relationships with their parents, teachers, employers, and friends. The course continues normally for 4 weeks and the group does not exceed 15. In fact, we prefer a maximum of 12. One of the sessions is given over to the facts of life, and young people are genuinely interested and ask a lot of questions on all kinds of misconceptions that they have about sex. Contraceptives are discussed and premarital intercourse is one of the vital things they want to talk about.

We do not have any Brook Advisory Clinics in Northern Ireland as yet but I feel we are just on the threshold of introducing them. Young people should be helped, ideally by their parents, but if this is not possible or advisable, by an adult who is sufficiently interested in them to discuss all the disadvantages and the few advantages of premarital sex. However, as Alan Ingleby in his book *Learning to Love* has said: 'In the last analysis people must be free to do what they honestly think is right, even if it goes against the society to which they belong.'

Are we perhaps too greatly preoccupied with a morality which measures chastity in terms of whether or not full sexual intercourse takes place, and too little in terms of those qualities of care and consideration, unselfishness and kindness, loyalty and integrity, without which no true chastity exists?

In Northern Ireland, in 1960, we ran groups with 300 young people. Last year, 1967, 1804 young people attended discussions. Counsellors trained to work with young people as well as to deal with marriage problems have more than trebled in the past 10 years. This in itself is a very healthy sign and I am sure you will agree that one of the community needs for family planning services is the provision of adequate education for family life.

THE CHAIRMAN: Thank you, Mrs. Greeves, for a very stimulating and instructive talk.

Now, ladies and gentlemen, we come to the part of this programme where you, the audience, will participate. We have had some interesting papers and many questions have been put to us. We have learned a lot from the speakers this morning that we had not known before. Some of the information we have received is quite startling. The remainder of this morning's programme rests with you and we now invite your questions and your comments.

DISCUSSION AT MORNING SESSION

THE CHAIRMAN: Perhaps it would be desirable if at this stage I asked Dr. Bamber, the County Medical Officer of Health for County Antrim, to come up and speak to us.

DR. W. BAMBER: Mr. Chairman, ladies, and gentlemen, I would first of all like personally to congratulate the authors of the papers on their most instructive papers and the admirable way in which they have been presented. I am afraid that I could not approach such eloquence at all, but I feel that in the public health field we are responsible for community health, and in the past we have been chiefly concerned with prevention of disease. We have still a lot of problems in the way of infectious diseases like food poisoning and tuberculosis, the latter still with us. But we have now reached the time when we can give more time to this question of the promotion of health, and if we are to promote the health of the community we will have to concern ourselves with family welfare, and that is very much concerned with this question of family planning. If the members of the family are to be healthy the family must essentially be an economic, stable unit in the community. Without family planning this cannot be.

First of all, if there are too many children some of them are going to be deprived if the father and mother, and particularly the mother, is not in the best of health. Obviously she cannot do her best for her family because she cannot give them all the attention she should. There is the other attitude that if there is family planning rather than contraception, then the numbers in the family can be regulated and arranged to suit the family. For all these reasons family planning seems to me to be an essential public health matter.

Certainly family doctors have a job to do in this field. In my day in medical school I am afraid this subject was not even touched on, but today students get some instruction in this subject. Here we should pay tribute to the Family Planning Association for the courses which it runs to instruct doctors in this important subject. I think it is admirable work that the Family Planning Association is doing.

As I have said, we have had most instructive papers. I would also pay tribute to the very informative paper we have had from Dr. Edgar. In his paper he mentioned that they had gone into the schools and I should like to hear a little more on this subject if he has had any experience of this. I was very delighted to hear of the work of the Marriage Guidance Council, and I think we should have more publicity for the work being done by it. It could possibly give us much help in our problems connected with family planning. I should like to congratulate the speakers and say how much I have enjoyed the proceedings so far.

DR. W. EDGAR: There are two points I should like to reply to. The first one is a fundamental one—the lack of cover of this subject in the medical student curriculum. It is quite some summers since I was a medical undergraduate, and even in Edinburgh I cannot recall any part of my training relating to family planning. When I went back after the War to do my public health training I recall one lecture on this subject. Such was the secrecy about the whole thing that it is vividly impressed on my mind. I know that many medical schools now appreciate the need for this training not only for medical students but increasingly in courses for health visitors and midwives, and they include this as an important and essential part of the training given. We have not gone far enough yet, because the subject of family planning is not merely a question of dispensing pills; it is a very personal thing and it is a very wide field. One has to have some knowledge and a degree of competence not only in the subject itself but also in dealing with people seeking such advice. We have a lot of progress to make, particularly in the undergraduate curriculum.

The other point was about the secondary modern, grammar, and technical schools. About three months ago I received a letter from the Principal of a technical college in which he said that there had been a demand from the students for a talk on the subject of venereal disease. I thought this was an important opening and that people in my position cannot refuse such opportunities. I discussed with the principal and the lecturer in social studies what the youngsters wanted as well as learning what sort of course was provided for them. As a result we held three talks and discussions. At the one yesterday we considered the effect of venereal disease, premarital intercourse, and family planning. I asked these youngsters what knowledge they had of any of these subjects and the answer was almost none. I asked them whether their parents had mentioned any of these subjects to them and the answer was in the negative. I then asked them whether they thought these subjects should be brought to their attention at this time or whether an earlier approach should be made, and they all felt, without exception, that they should have known about this before leaving school. That is my own personal experience in this technical college, but I should like to emphasize that if the opportunity were offered to me by the headmaster or headmistress of any secondary school I would take it. A competent woman member of my staff talks regularly in senior schools on the subject of sex education and she deals with this subject of family planning also. It is important because children at this stage are forming their own minds, their own standards, their own attitudes, and it is only right that they should have the appropriate and correct information.

MRS. T. GREEVES: Publicity for the work of the Marriage Guidance Council was mentioned by Dr. Bamber and I should like to deal briefly with that. I suppose basically we do not do very much publicity for the one big reason that we have very little money. We get a Government grant as well as a grant from the Corporation, for which we are very grateful. We also get grants from local authorities but not nearly enough. We do get a little publicity and the newspapers are usually very good. It might surprise this audience to know that the Northern Ireland Marriage Guidance Council was formed in 1947, which is 21 years ago, and it is rather frightening that an Ulster audience like this does not know about us.

THE CHAIRMAN: We know about you but we do not know enough about you.

MRS. T. GREEVES: We have a number of counsellors, about 24, and most of them are spending their time either on marriage counselling or on educational work. Normally they are people who are doing a full-time job and they do this in the evening although some counsellors are available during the day. One must remember that they are all voluntary workers. We are glad of the opportunity to talk to rotary clubs, women's institutes, and such-like bodies, and we encourage such clubs to be interested in our work. However, we do not like to use our skilled workers to do this kind of work, although most of them do it. But this is just one of our difficulties. We want them to do the work for which they were trained rather than go out and talk. We are extremely fortunate that we have been able to appoint Mr. David Vandeleur as the first-ever executive officer, and this is the kind of thing that he intends to do.

We could do with a lot more publicity for the Marriage Guidance Council. I realize that people do not know enough about us and they know nothing about our educational work. This, of course, is because of our name. They think that marriage guidance is remedial work; they have never heard of our educational work, and, quite frankly, I am slightly biased because I am much more interested in the educational work. I think we will always continue with our remedial work because it will always be necessary, but one hopes that with more education about family life it will not be as necessary.

I would be very grateful if any member of the audience could suggest ways in which we could get publicity. The Press are very good, at times, in giving publicity to our work, and if we do not make the headlines we do get some publicity for our meetings. If any members of the audience— and I will throw this back to you—have any suggestions to make which would make for improvement in the public image of the Marriage Guidance Council I would be delighted to get those suggestions.

A MEMBER OF THE AUDIENCE suggested that the clergy of all types could help, as they were almost in competition with the council.

MRS. GREEVES replied: It is true that the clergy work closely with us, and we meet them in our house on the Dublin Road. The clergy are one body that ought to know a lot about us because many of them send us clients. They are very helpful and sympathetic, I agree.

THE CHAIRMAN: I have been handed a question from Dr. G. P. M. Marshall, of Coleraine, and I will read it to you. It is: 'In view of the many cases of repeated illegitimacy and consequent grossly inefficient social and moral upbringing of children, why is birth control by the Northern Ireland Family Planning Association restricted to those who are married?'

I think this is a question that can best be dealt with by Mrs. Betty Hunter, of the Brook Advisory Centres. We are very fortunate to have Mrs. Hunter with us. She is the National Organizer of Brook Advisory Centres and in answering this question I am sure she will tell us something about her organization and its great work.

MRS. B. HUNTER: Mr. Chairman, ladies, and gentlemen, I think it is time we had some fireworks in the meeting and here I am ready to be shot at. Just in case anyone in the room is not aware of the function of the Brook Advisory Centres I should just like to say that we started our first London clinic in 1964 for the purpose of giving contraception advice to the unmarried. When our work began that was considered a very radical thing to do. But as the speakers have said this morning, public opinion in England and Wales has changed considerably during the 4 years that our organization has been operating. We have seen an Act of Parliament last year—the National Health Service (Family Planning) Act 1967—which it is true is only permissive, but it does not differentiate between the married and the unmarried. It merely says that contraceptive help may be given to women. That, I think, is the most important aspect of the problem.

Brook Advisory Centres were set up as a voluntary organization because, as we all know, any controversial matters of this nature have to be started through the initiative of a few voluntary workers at the beginning. We began with one small clinic in London. We now have two clinics in London, one in Cambridge, one in Birmingham, one in Bristol, one in Liverpool, another in Birkenhead, one in Edinburgh, and I hope, very shortly, that we shall have one in Glasgow. So we are gradually expanding throughout the country.

In England and Wales the Family Planning Association took the national decision to see the unmarried in their clinics provided that there was a local clinic willing to do this. Consequently some family planning clinics, of which there are over 700 in England and Wales, are, in fact, seeing the unmarried. But still there are many areas of the country where it is not possible for unmarried people to get help and advice of the kind that is needed. The Brook clinics will see any girl or boy aged 16 years or over, but when I say age 16 do not imagine that we have queues of grammar school children lined up wanting contraceptives. We see very few patients in the age-group 16–18. In fact only 10 per cent of those coming to us are under 18 years of age. The bulk of those visiting our clinics are those of 19 and 20 and up to 25. To some of our clinics older people are sent, but in London it is restricted to 25. These young people who come to us are not virgins; they are having sexual intercourse quite regularly with a steady partner. Ten per cent of those who come to us have had an illegitimate baby or an abortion; they are people who are very seriously at risk. We do not moralize about their conduct. Their conduct is their own personal decision. The people coming to us are seeking advice and help and they are adopting a responsible attitude to sex. Our organization is there to help them with advice.

Ours are not 'pill-dispensing shops'. It is a responsible service conducted by members with family planning training. They also help some of these young people with their emotional problems. Because they do have, in many cases, feelings of guilt about their course of conduct they have all sorts of worries and other problems which they should be discussing with their own parents. Many find that they cannot talk to their parents or even to their family practitioner about these things. When these young people come to an impersonal medical person at a Brook clinic they find that they can talk much more easily. One is able in the course of their visits to the clinic over the year for medical checks and supplies to assist these people so that the worries and difficulties which bewilder them can be worked out.

Before I say anything more I should like to deal with the question from the audience that the Chairman read out. Some of you will be thinking that we are doing something we ought not to be doing. I am not here to argue on the morals; we are tackling a job that has to be done. Perhaps we ought to have a clinic in Northern Ireland or, indeed, more than one clinic, and we need more than a handful of clinics in England and Wales, but until we get some more money we will struggle along in our small way.

MISS DAVIS: In the face of all this promiscuity is there really any need for marriage at all?

MRS. B. HUNTER: I am afraid I could not attempt to answer that question. Unfortunately some promiscuity is there. People are not behaving as they used to. As Mrs. Brook said on one occasion, she did not invent sex; it has always been there but she brought it into the open and tried to do something to prevent illegitimate births. Nothing is more tragic than an unwanted child starting off with all the disadvantages which Dr. Edgar has mentioned. Surely one must not think of the moral issues entirely but should also think of the social aspects, and particularly of the child who is unwanted, unloved, and is thrown on the scrap heap of human life. Some advice from an organization like Brook Centres could well have prevented its being born.

MISS DAVIS: But if the panel are in favour of the Brook clinics how do Mrs. Hunter and her colleagues know that their clinics will not increase promiscuity by being the means of removing the threat from such conduct? I am sure that is often the position.

MRS. B. HUNTER: As I have said, the people who come to us are already having intercourse. Some of you might consider these people are pro-miscuous, but surely if anyone is having intercourse outside marriage then the question of birth control is more important than is the case when they are married.

THE CHAIRMAN: We are concerned at present with the increase in venereal disease amongst young people. The statistics for Northern Ireland show a similar trend to the statistics in Britain. In Belfast we have begun to take this thing so seriously—the Ministry, too, have been worried about it—that we have a full-time health visitor working entirely on this subject of venereal disease, mostly in young people. Surely clinics like yours, Mrs. Hunter, unless there is very, very careful supervision—and I do not know the details of how many people you have visiting them—will tend to increase venereal disease rather than help us to cut it down, largely through increasing promiscuity.

MRS. B. HUNTER: We see very few cases of venereal disease in our clinics. In fact, in the clinic in London where I have my office the clinical secretary came to me very recently and told me: 'We have had our first case of venereal disease.' That is in a clinic that has been operating for $2\frac{1}{2}$ years. We are now seeing something like 2000–3000 new patients there each year; one cannot say what the figures will be later on. As you have said, Mr. Chairman, this does appear to be an increasing trend among young people, but the young people who come to us are having steady relationships; they are not sleeping here and there with anyone. They very often get married and we transfer about 500 patients a year following marriage to Family Planning Associations. We have very few problems with venereal disease and all our patients are examined by a doctor on their first visit. If there is any suspicion of V.D. it is checked straightaway. When such patients come back on their next visit, they are again seen by a doctor and medically examined, and that continues for the time that is thought necessary.

MRS. T. GREEVES: I do not know enough about this subject to speak on it, but I was wondering about the young woman who has not quite made up her mind about wanting to use contraceptives or, indeed, having pre-marital intercourse. She is troubled and worried about it and she is anxious to talk to a consultant and discuss the whole problem with such a person.

MRS. B. HUNTER: There are always some girls who come for a discussion and go away to think about the advice given to them. But we see very few virgins. Those who are already having intercourse usually go away with contraceptives. I should mention that, following the practice in the Family Planning Council, if we prescribe oral contraceptives we always refer to the girl's own doctor to see if there are any medical reasons why this should not be given. The medical practitioner can cause difficulties if he refuses consent, perhaps on moral grounds. Then we have to recommend some other form of contraception.

DR. J. WILSON: If this promiscuity can be prevented, why not prevent it as a community by education and such means? Surely it is a terrible thing to think of this increased promiscuity and the spread of venereal disease, a great deal of it caused by people having relationships outside marriage?

THE CHAIRMAN: I think that is more a moral problem, and I do not know whether Mrs. Hunter would care to deal with it.

MRS. B. HUNTER: I think this is something we can never prevent. Probably Mrs. Greeves would be able to say a little more about the sex educational programmes for young people. These I feel do not start at an early enough stage. Usually sex instruction in schools begins in the 12–14 age-groups. My personal opinion is that this should start much earlier when the children can absorb it without sniggering, carrying out experiments, and that sort of thing.

MRS. T. GREEVES: We start normally with the 13–14 age-groups. I would emphasize that we do not really provide sex education We give a course on personal relations, and one of the issues is the facts of life. We talk about them and we are always amazed at the number of questions asked afterwards. The young people are searching for an answer to their problems, and they will say, 'Right, what do you think of premarital intercourse?' and you will tell them what are the principles of the Marriage Guidance Council in the matter. Quite often they accept that, but sometimes they will ask, 'But what do you feel?' Quite frankly, my answer to this has always been that it is not for me to tell anybody what is right and what is wrong. This is something that each young person must decide for himself or herself. You give them the facts, you tell them what you consider are the disadvantages of premarital sex and the advantages of restraint, and in the last analysis you leave it to him or her to decide.

THE CHAIRMAN: This brings me to something I might mention. You may have seen the programme on television with Alan Whicker entitled *Whicker's World*, which was screened about a month ago. It dealt with the question of promiscuity, and Whicker interviewed young women from three different social levels in life. The third was a young girl from a factory in Nottingham, and I think we all know which factory it was. He had this most frank interview with the young lady. He got her talking and at the end of the programme, when discussing very personal things, he asked her had she ever had relations with a man and she said, 'Of course, yes I have.' He further said to her, 'How many girls in your factory do you think are virgins?', and she replied, 'I don't think there are any.' That was the answer to the question, and on this level of promiscuity this was her opinion. It might not be far away from the truth in the younger age-groups so that the type of clinic like the Brook clinics will be necessary in the future. I feel that this was a very vital question put by Dr. Wilson. It would almost appear as if we must start an approach to young people to prevent this promiscuity. We must face that fact.

MRS. B. HUNTER: I think we must.

DR. J. NEILL: I think we are using 'promiscuity' wrongly. Mrs. Hunter says that the people who visit her clinics are having steady relations, and these girls in this Nottingham factory are not necessarily promiscuous. That they have been sleeping with boys is a moral concern and we may disagree with them in that. The really promiscuous are possibly the result of what is known as a psychopathic personality or because they have some other difficulty. This situation is much more a matter of personal relations—something for which we have to work out a scheme for those in need.

DR. J. WILSON: Could we not run classes for parents and try to do more in the early stages and not leave so much actually to people like our panel and to teachers? I think much of the trouble comes from neglect by the parents. Could more not be done in the early stages?

MRS. T. GREEVES: I could not agree with you more. I know that the parents are the people to do this sort of thing. I think that if some of them feel they cannot do it then we possibly could help by getting our counsellors to spend a certain amount of time preparing parents to accept this responsibility. I should have said we have literature for parents to help them to talk to their children about the facts of life right from an early age. About 5 years ago I had a survey made and one thing that surprised me was that out of 500 young people to whom I spoke over a period of 2 years—and this 500 was drawn from all strata of society—only 2 had been told anything about the facts of life by their parents. In every group in that survey the youngsters said that they would have liked their parents to have told them from the beginning. I know it is difficult.

It was suggested that the time was ripe to run groups for parents. We have in the past run groups on housing estates, in connexion with parents' associations, and sometimes in parent-teacher associations in schools. In this way we have been in contact with parents, and I would just add that if the parents could do this it would be a tremendous help and the young people would certainly appreciate it. I also think there comes a stage with these young people when it is not so easy to get across to them. I am noticing it with my own children. My eldest has reached the age of 15, the stage when he really thinks I am an absolute square and that I do not know anything. We have reached this awful stage when he simply will not talk to me about these things and when I attempt to talk to him he is not interested. I know a lot of other parents worry about this. They say they can talk to their children until about the 13 or 14 age-groups and then they have their emotional period and the parents just cannot get through to their children. I understand when they are 20 years of age they start talking to you again, but I will have to wait a long time until that happens with me.

DR. J. B. McKINNEY: What facilities are available for in-service training of doctors and other staff employed by public health departments, including family planning clinics? Are these facilities adequate and if not what are we in Northern Ireland doing in this field?

THE CHAIRMAN: I should say in regard to that question that this will be discussed in the papers this afternoon, but perhaps Dr. Neill might like to say something now.

DR. J. NEILL: The situation about the training of doctors in family planning is that we have run one course of lectures in conjunction with the Post Graduate Medical School. This was over a year ago and I do not know when we will manage to run another one, so that at the moment we are working with the Family Planning Association. Over many years it has done very good training courses in a couple of days' lectures and some practical training, which for doctors means six visits to our clinic and for nurses eight visits. We have two training clinics in Northern Ireland which are recognized by the English Family Planning Association towards their certificate. We hope to have more clinics, but at the moment that is the position. The only way to attend another lecture course such as I mentioned at the beginning is to go across to England for one of the Family Planning Association's lecture courses. We may possibly be able to arrange another course of lectures here, particularly if people are interested and there are enough coming forward for it. The one that was run by the Post Graduate Medical School was very well attended by a lot of public health personnel, both doctors and nurses.

DR. G. RAMAGE: I have some facts about the training courses run by the Family Planning Association but these are purely concerned with England and Wales. I thought, however, that they would be of interest. In 1966 its courses were attended by 211 doctors and 372 nurses, of whom 45 and 20 respectively were from abroad. The courses were concerned with contraceptive practices and with the insertion of I.U.D.s. A total of 260 doctors gained the certificate of competence which is available to any general practitioner who attends a recognized clinic and this involves a minimum attendance of four sessions.

THE CHAIRMAN: There will probably be an extension of this in the afternoon. I have here a question from Councillor J. R. Davis, a member of Londonderry County Health Committee. This question is not entirely relevant to our discussion, but perhaps we might get a quick answer from the panel. I do not think we should permit discussion on it any longer because it is not strictly relevant. The question is: 'Should people of low intelligence be forbidden to marry?'

DR. G. RAMAGE: The simple answer is that I know of no legal procedure which prohibits such a person marrying. There is no procedure of any kind which can restrict their activities in that direction. There can be a similar problem with the mentally subnormal, particularly when hostels are provided. Training them to conform is much more difficult than is the training of persons whose mental ability is normal. There is no law which can prevent such people marrying and the suggestion we have before us is quite impractical.

DR. W. EDGAR: The only additional comment I can make is that if they

4

do marry consultant obstetricians are concerned about this problem, and where there is agreement with the patients they do recommend sterilization.

DR. McLOUGHLIN: I am old fashioned enough to believe that fear is a very important factor in the development of the race and the units within the race. After all, it is fear that keeps a child from getting burnt. It is fear that keeps us all from being road casualties. It is fear which prevents the nations going to war. In this very permissive society of ours we have here something which I think could go a considerable distance to remove fear. These centres about which we have heard could make it easier to be promiscuous and that is something to be deplored. After all, if we are trying to educate people to uphold moral standards and at the same time making it easy without any risk of penalty to transgress moral standards I think we are being inconsistent. I should like to know, for example in this audience, what would be the consensus of opinion for and against such centres.

DR. G. RAMAGE: If I could I should like to make one comment at this stage. When we are providing contraceptives and giving advice on the subject—and this is part of what I shall be talking about this afternoon—we must remember that we are only putting women in the same position as men have been for years. They can henceforth with a reliable method engage in intercourse without the penalty of pregnancy, and that has been the exact situation in which men have been from the very beginning. Why should the women be subject to fear and not the men?

DR. HALL: I am a member of one of the group practices in Belfast. I want to make this comment. Someone on the platform said that they were surprised that one-third of the girls on their wedding day were pregnant. My partner and I attend about 250 maternity cases in the year and we do a lot of gynaecology and obstetrics and I am not surprised at those statistics at all. Recently a number of women who had children stated to me that they were prepared to sign a letter with their husbands agreeing to sterilization. Shortly after that and within the past 4 weeks, three men came to me and said they were not prepared to have their wives sterilized but that they would be happy to have themselves sterilized. I wonder whether the platform would care to comment on sterilization.

DR. G. RAMAGE: It is a little bit off my line but I have some information here which may be of interest to you. The Simon Population Trust have organized a project to facilitate the use of sterilization as a contraceptive method. Anyone wishing to undergo sterilization should consult their general practitioner who will refer them to a surgeon of their choice. Guidance for the general practitioner on this subject, or the names of surgeons willing to undertake the operation, can be obtained from Mrs. Avant, Secretary, 'Longsight', Crediton, Devon. The Director of the project is Dr. L. N. Jackson and literature is available from her for patients whose doctors are in doubt or opposed to sterilization on religious or other grounds.

The inquiries received regarding sterilization are steadily increasing and come mostly from men, for whom the operation is much simpler than for women, who are dissatisfied with contraceptive devices or have found them unreliable. The majority are in the age-group 30–40 with two or more children, and close in numbers to these is the age-group 20–30 with three or more children. The precise number of men whom the Trust has helped is not known, but up to July, 1967, 1000 had undergone vaso-ligation.

The safeguards laid down by the Medical Defence Union are scrupulously observed, that is, the co-operation of the general practitioner and a consent form by both spouses, which makes the operation perfectly legal. Postoperatively sperm counts are essential and should start 8 weeks after the operation. No diminution of potency occurs, nor is there any adverse effect on sexual life. Indeed the freedom from the possibility of pregnancy results in quite the reverse.

I agree that this is not an exact reply to the question but I think it contains material which may be of interest.

THE CHAIRMAN: I had the privilege of being in India for 6 weeks in January and February, and I took the opportunity in Bombay and in Madras and Calcutta to see something of family planning. Indeed the Indian Government are approaching this largely through sterilization and they make a payment of a pound to each male who comes in and is sterilized. Unfortunately the scheme is not working out as well as was expected. This question of potency, which Dr. Ramage mentioned, is uppermost with the men, but it is absolutely true to say, as he did, that there is no diminution of potency following this, but only the psychological effect of vasectomy which sometimes leads to a problem of potency.

The second point I wanted to make was that some clinics are set up at railway stations. Many thousands of people pass through the railway stations and the clinics are on the platform. They get this pound payment and I asked about it. I was told that it was not payment and this was emphasized most emphatically. The authorities say that this is to compensate the man for 2 days' pay which he loses following the operation.

AFTERNOON SESSION

THE CHAIRMAN: This afternoon we have Dr. Ramage as speaker. He is Medical Officer of Health for Staffordshire and is actively engaged in supporting family planning and has been since way back immediately after the War. He was a member of the working party on Family Planning Reorganization and since 1952 his local authority, the Staffordshire Local Health Authority, has supported family planning in the county and clinics have been set up numbering eight at the moment. Another point I should like to mention is that his authority contributed more money per clinic than any other authority in Britain. Through Dr. Ramage's keenness this work is going ahead quickly in his county. I have much pleasure in calling on Dr. Ramage.

ORGANIZING THE CLINIC

G. RAMAGE

MR. CHAIRMAN, ladies, and gentlemen, thank you for the very pleasant introduction. The subject we are discussing now is one in which I have taken a very close interest. In fact, I look on the subject of family planning, possibly allied to health education, as the most important work that the health committees are engaged in.

We are talking this afternoon about the organizing of the clinic but I hope you will not expect me to stay within the four walls of the clinic. Actually the clinic is the subject for a later speaker, while I propose to talk about the administrative approach towards starting a clinic and organizing a family planning scheme.

Here we must ask ourselves the question, once the committees agree to look at a scheme, for what are we organizing the clinic? We are organizing for family planning as defined this morning; family planning being intended to enable people to regulate their fertility as far as they wish. Therefore in any of our county clinics—and naturally I speak largely from my own experience in my own area—we would require to include subfertility clinics and we would not wish clinics to be run purely on birth-control lines. Although Professor Pinkerton did remark that in the passage of time this has become a large part of family planning, as local authorities we are not concerned with population control. Population control has different criteria and is not our object, though, of course, we may help in population control if that is thought desirable by the Government.

It has been said several times that family planning is nothing new, that we have had it for quite a long time. Most authorities have been providing services, either directly or indirectly, by helping the Family Planning Association and voluntary bodies. The circular which the Ministry issued 2 years ago, that is, Circular 5/1966, changed the atmosphere from one of almost back-door diplomacy in getting clinics going to open discussion. More than this, it has changed the Ministry's official conception which started way back in 1931, that of birth control for women in local authority clinics to family planning for the population as a whole. The situation is infinitely easier and, of course, the field is much wider.

DIRECT ADMINISTRATION OR SERVICE AGENCY

When organizing the clinic the first job one has to do is to obtain committee decisions on matters of principle before the Family Planning Association is approached or organization of a directly run clinic starts.

The first of these questions is whether the service should be a local health association providing direct service or whether it should be provided through an agent. There are a number of independent clinics and a large number of family planning clinics; for example, we had an excellent account this morning of the Brook clinics. Ultimately all authorities will wish to administer these services directly because the circular accompanying the Act (15/67) makes it clear that family planning is to be part of the health services, and it cannot really be so if run by some independent body and the remainder of the services are the direct responsibility of the health committees.

For the time being, however, in England and Wales it may be more effective to use the existing pattern of clinics to fulfil the Act and the accompanying circular. I say this because a number of authorities are not ready for a 100 per cent service organized in the way the Minister wishes and we must take our authorities with us by a gradual process.

Then, authorities may have difficulties in staffing if they try to provide a direct service. Nurses are required and the opening of the clinics is often outside normal hours. Voluntary workers at the clinics are helping without any payment or their payment is very small and intended merely to cover their expenses. The service would, in fact, be more expensive for the local authority if the volunteers did not continue. I think it is less likely that they would continue if the clinics are taken over by the local authorities and run directly. Finally, a number of family planning branches have their own premises and these would continue even if the local authority organized their own clinics, so it is obviously economic that existing premises should be used.

SCOPE OF THE SERVICE

The range of the service that the local authority will provide must be decided in advance. There might be a difference of opinion between the local authority and the voluntary bodies about this. Such as disagreement on giving advice to the unmarried. It is much more likely that the local authority would not wish as wide a service as the voluntary societies would wish to give. Failure to agree on such things as advice to the unmarried might prevent an agency arrangement or at least result in the voluntary society continuing independently to provide that part of the service which the local authority would not accept.

A fundamental point to be decided is to whom the advice shall be offered. Hitherto family planning has very largely been a woman's organization. Now the word 'persons' is used in the Act, and obviously this includes men as well as women. The main controversy is on the giving of a contraceptive service to the unmarried, and the associated question at what age this should be given. The latter point is tied up with the need for parental consent which local authority cannot disregard. They carefully observe it in their handling of schoolchildren and of handicapped schoolchildren.

I will not repeat what has been so ably said this morning about the pros and cons of providing a service for the unmarried. It is up to us to persuade our own authorities if we feel that it is right and it may well be that the authorities will insist on it themselves. My own authority, who for many years have been accustomed to help the Family Planning Association, had no hesitation in saying that a service should be provided. Public opinion and newspaper publicity seemed to have a clear effect in persuading them to this conclusion, but they put in a stipulation—that no unmarried person under 18 should be seen or given advice without parental consent. At first sight this seemed a reasonable restriction but in practice it means that nobody under 19 will attend county-supported clinics. It may be that the Brook clinic in Birmingham, about which you have already heard, will be the means of providing this service, which we cannot provide.

In this matter I suggested to the committee that no advice should be given to anyone under 16 without consultation with the county medical officer. We do not anticipate many so young cases and any which come forward will be those already known to the authority either through the probation officer or through the children's officer. Nevertheless, it is a useful reserve to have up one's sleeve for the really difficult, incurable young person.

In advising the unmarrieds the county authority has stipulated that an advisory service shall always be available. This, I think, is the key to whether one should or should not advise the unmarried. I have heard of more than one instance where a young unmarried person has gone to a clinic for advice and after discussion has said, 'No, I do not want the preventive now, thank you.' So a service to the unmarried can serve that purpose too, and we are aiming to help people to form their own judgements, which is much preferable to compulsion.

RELATIONSHIP TO OTHER LOCAL AUTHORITY CLINICS

Another point to decide is the relationship in terms of time and geography to other activities run by the local authority, such as maternity and child welfare clinics held in local authority premises. In this respect I think it is interesting to read what Marie Stopes, who is now considered a heroine rather than a reprobate, said in 1922: 'I did not then and I do not now consider that more birth control clinics as independent institutions should be the answer. The obvious proper place to obtain contraceptive advice is in the ante-natal clinics and the infant welfare clinics of the hospitals.' That was in 1922 and we are now 40 years on and seeing the acceptance of this idea. Nevertheless, because of the varying size of buildings and the number of clinics required, family planning clinics must be fitted in. Some must be held in the evenings, if only to bring the husbands into the picture. They are concerned in two ways: they can stay at home and look after the children while mother attends; or they themselves can come and take part in the discussion on the methods to be used. Possibly some of them may themselves wish to go further and take the burden of prevention from their wives, as was discussed this morning.

Whether there should be a separate session for the unmarried has, I think, got to find its own level. It will depend on the numbers that attend in proportion to the married women and on the population density. In some cases unmarrieds have attended with the married and there has been no objection. It seems likely that we shall not organize separate clinics specially because people are unmarried, but it may be for other reasons that they will be established.

THE PART OF THE LOCAL HEALTH AUTHORITY STAFF IN FAMILY PLANNING WORK

The circular to local authorities which accompanied the new Act stresses almost in every line that family planning was to be looked upon from now on as being as much a part of the local authority service as the ambulance service and the midwifery service, the home-help service, and every other service in the scheme. When Sir Theodore Fox came to Staffordshire to talk to our staff he said this: 'A social worker in the field is working with one arm tied behind her back without using family planning facilities.'

So in the start of any new family planning scheme or in any enlargement of an existing scheme at an early date the health visitors, the midwives, the nurses, and the social workers should be called together and given the outline of the programme that is to be carried out. They must first of all be informed of the council's policy because the council's policy might not be 100 per cent of what is recommended by the Ministry. They must also have practical details of the way the service is running; where it is available; how far they are expected to take part. And, finally, they must have it firmly put to them that family planning is part of their work.

In carrying out this we must have regard to the attitude which the Ministry expressed in 1931 when family planning was much more controversial, although they have not repeated their advice. They then said (Circular 1208 14/7/31, para. 5) that any medical officer should be free to undertake or decline to work as his convictions dictated. We have adopted this, but it has been laid down by a resolution of our committee and now passed by the council that any person joining the service in future shall undertake to regard family planning as part of his or her duty. So as time goes on we shall have a staff which we can expect and require to work with family planning. This is a key point.

The health visitors are particularly important in this service because in England and Wales—I am not sure what the arrangements are here in Northern Ireland—they are the only local authority official who has reason to go into every home. Because of this and their nursing qualifications, the health visitors are ideal people to help with family planning for the benefits of the individuals we have been talking about.

DOMICILIARY SCHEMES

I am not going to talk about this in detail but we should look on it as a last resort. In my own area we have the experience of our health visitors bringing people to the clinics and we would like the next stage of persuasion, if it is required, to be a kind of domiciliary service, a service where the doctor, as well as the nurse, would try to exert more pressure so that the person shall come to the clinic. Finally, if this fails the doctor and nurse must do the best they can under the domestic conditions prevailing.

COST OF FAMILY PLANNING

The question of costs unfortunately loom very large at the present time. There is no doubt whatever that any sum of money we can spend on family planning eventually is going to give us a twentyfold return (one need only consider the cost referred to by Dr. Edgar when he set out the number of children in care and the cash saving possible through family planning). Money should not matter in family planning, but at the moment we must go quietly and expense is the determining factor in expansion.

The Minister stated in his circular which accompanied the Act that he would approve charges for prescriptions, supplies, drugs, and appliances in non-medical cases only. This really infuriates a lot of people. This distinction between medical and non-medical cases was made in 1924 as a sop to the opponents of family planning; it was perpetuated in the circular which started family planning in 1931, and we had all hoped that the distinction had been decently buried, but now it has been raised again. All these years we have taken the view that if a woman was in fear of further pregnancies that would be detrimental to her health, she was entitled to treatment. Yet here again we have this distinction raised. This could be used by the reluctant local authorities to reduce their service.

The Minister is saying really that the service should be free with small exceptions. I advised the committee from the beginning that I thought this was not a sound procedure. I doubt if society should be asked to pay for what is a convenience to an individual in the absence of a population control policy.

How much the scheme is going to cost is very difficult to estimate. I have some figures with me but they would not be of much value because circumstances differ in each area. Much depends on the extent of the use of voluntary workers. Although volunteers do work in Government-maintained services (e.g., Friends of the Hospital) they do so more willingly in a voluntary society. Now in England we have a new factor in that the Government has changed its mind and has decided to make charges for prescriptions, so for the moment there is rather a swing towards making charges.

As a matter of interest, in my own county when the health committee was considering first of all, having a free service, it was found that on the previous year's figures, if charges were eliminated in accordance with the Minister's proposal the county would need to pay another £9000 per year. This gives an idea of the large sums involved over the whole country.

INTEGRATION OF THE SERVICE

I should now like to say a few words about the integration of the service. The needs of family planning should be kept in mind in the design of all clinics; no clinic from now on should be erected without consideration of where the family planning sessions can be held. As we build more and more health centres with plenty of room no special problem will arise, but in smaller buildings this need should not be lost sight of.

It was said this morning that family planning was becoming more and more clinical and more and more a medical matter. There is no doubt that ultimately family planning will form part of the general integration which is now happily taking place in England and Wales. When the organization of the health centres is provided by the local health committee and the ancillary aid to relieve doctors in their routine work is available, general practitioners will have more time to give to clinical work, including family planning. One factor here of importance is that voluntary bodies and the local health authorities have more time available at present than the general practitioners, and for people visiting the family planning clinics it should not be a matter of just getting contraceptives or being issued with the pill. Rather these visits are an occasion when the woman can free herself from some psychological difficulties as well as receive physical attention. She should also be given an unhurried and sympathetic reception. If these matters are not arranged then much of the value of the clinic is being lost. Therefore for a longish time to come we shall see the family planning clinics continuing as separate organizations until we reach that happy day when the general practitioner's time is not spent on less important matters and we have group practices where the doctors can make this a task of their own and give it the time that it requires.

I must mention the relationship of the clinic to the general practitioner on clinical grounds. The Ministry and the Family Planning Association feel that before a woman begins receiving a contraceptive pill or an I.U.D. there should be a consultation with the general practitioner. As a doctor myself I applaud this; as a citizen I have a few lingering doubts. Certainly it should never be done without the woman's permission. I feel that the freedom of action by the woman is her right as a citizen. So any comment that a general practitioner makes—and I refer to this rather delicately— should be on purely medical grounds. I know there are a lot of medical practitioners here so I pass on just saying that this is a thought which must be expressed.

With regard to relationships with the hospital, this subject was dealt with this morning by Professor Pinkerton. I fully endorse his remarks about clinics and hospitals. There is one matter which has not been mentioned which we have found useful; that is genetic assessments.

PRACTICAL POINTS

Turning now to practical issues the committee will want to be satisfied that the clinics are conveniently situated to the population, the times of opening being reasonable and sufficient. We also want to ensure good publicity so that the public clearly knows where to go. The medical officer of health and the authority will want to know more than this, such as the suitability of the rooms used and a harmonious relationship between the volunteer workers and the permanent staff, if local authority premises are used. In the past the voluntary people have been looked on by some of the permanent staff as intruders.

As regards the efficiency of the service, the medical officer of health will want to know the average time of waiting of people who come to the clinic, also the length of waiting lists and, in particular, what is the waiting list for I.U.D. He should be interested in a confidential environment within the clinic to ensure that the patients are at ease, and he should also be concerned with the maintenance of an advisory service. Reference has been made to marriage guidance in appropriate cases, with the point about sub-fertility, clinical smears, and the availability of advice to husbands.

The actual annual numbers of patients dealt with can be extracted from the family planning clinic annual report and the medical officer of health can see from his own observations whether the right people are going to the clinics or not. This is an important point because those going tend to be non-manual people and this has been a criticism of family planning, though I never regarded it as such. A voluntary body providing a service in spite of criticism and ignorance could only deal with the enlightened woman. In the form which the Family Planning Association uses there is a space for the husband's occupation so that the social classes attending are known, and these useful statistics can be so arranged that they can be the means of showing whether we, in fact, are providing a service for a stratum of society which we feel most needs it.

Then, finally, the medical officer cannot dissociate himself from the fact that adequately trained staff are working in the clinic. The details on this are going to be dealt with by Dr. Neill, who no doubt will stress the importance of adequate supervision in pill cases and with the I.U.D. This is a matter of considerable concern to the local medical officer of health, and he cannot divest himself of a concern for procedure in the clinic.

THE CHAIRMAN: Thank you very much, Dr. Ramage, for the information that you have given to us. It will be of extreme value to those of us who will be setting up family planning clinics over here. This is bound to happen. I certainly feel that practices will be stimulated as a result of the papers we have heard today. In Northern Ireland we have had this distinction between medical and social cases. We follow step by step with Great Britain but this is one place where we are still a step behind.

Next we have Dr. Joyce Neill who has been a pioneer in family planning in Northern Ireland and who for many years has been closely associated with the Family Planning Association. She is now Chairman and I think that at present they are running about twelve clinics in Northern Ireland. Some are in local authority premises, while others are entirely organized by themselves without assistance from anybody. We look forward with interest to Dr. Neill's paper.

PATIENT COUNSELLING: TECHNIQUES AND MATERIALS AVAILABLE

J. G. NEILL

I WANT first to thank Ortho Pharmaceutical Limited for arranging this Conference because in the Family Planning Association we sometimes feel that we are labouring on but not publicizing the claims of family planning sufficiently. To have this get-together of local authority representatives, those from the Family Planning Associations, and the people from across the water who have more experience than we have is of great value to us. We are very grateful for this opportunity.

I have been asked to talk about the technique of counselling and the materials available. I do not know who chose this title, perhaps it was Professor Huntingford who talked about this subject at the London Conference. But it was handed to me and the more I have thought about it the wider its implications seem to be. I could, I think, speak for a good deal longer than my present time, if you were prepared to listen to me, and still leave a lot unexplored. However, I will try to highlight what I consider the important aspects of patient counselling and emphasize some of the special implications in Ulster.

The term 'counselling' is a relatively new one, borrowed, I think, from that border country between psychiatry and social work. Professor Halmos describes it as an attitude of caring, listening, and prompting, with, especially in the rather more superficial sense in which it is used sometimes in the United States, an additional offering of advice. The counselling approach to a patient, therefore, differs from the traditional doctor–patient interview, and this is the first thing I want to say. If a patient has, say, an acute appendicitis the doctor can say with some conviction, 'You must have an immediate operation or you may die.' The doctor knows and advises and the patient accepts and agrees. But in a situation such as a family planning interview when the patient comes asking for contraceptive advice the doctor can only say, 'You can do *a, b,* or *c,* but your marriage is special to you, and providing there are no medical reasons against any particular method, you must choose.' This involves some change in attitudes of patients and quite a lot of change on the doctor's part. He must be aware of his own attitudes to sex and marriage and try not to let them colour the interview. He must be sensitive to the patient's attitude to these things and be ready to hear the unasked question. The request for contraception may have been an excuse to discuss something else. The doctor must also somehow show his 'neutrality' so that the patient is able to talk on subjects not easily spoken of; and, finally, he must try to be aware of the effect of the patient on him and vice versa and use this knowledge.

So who does the counselling? Because whoever does must be prepared to acquire the necessary techniques both of counselling and the various methods of contraception. Just before answering this question, however, there is another question to be answered. Do we, in fact, need counsellors? This is worth looking at briefly because, consisting mostly as we do here of the converted, we have to remember that a number of people consider there are no problems about family planning. I was discussing this recently with someone who put forward this view: 'People can go to the chemist for the sheath or to their doctor for the pill.' Most people here, however, see the other side of the picture. They see many people who need at any rate some advice and help and I want to consider now who should give it.

The first and most obvious person is the family doctor. He knows the couple and the family situation better than anyone. This has been dealt with already today. Until recently not many medical schools taught family planning. But this position is improving and in any case for the general practitioner who wants to give advice there are good short postgraduate courses. Further, any general practitioner who has an interest in the subject can take the Family Planning Association's training which has been going for many years.

The second obvious group to give family planning advice is the obstetricians and the gynaecologists, but I am sorry to see that, with honourable exceptions, they seem a bit thin on the ground today. Perhaps they are too busy delivering babies to find time to come. *Apropos* of this I should like to tell you a short but revealing story. Two years ago I went to a conference of the I.P.P.F. in Copenhagen. Before the conference I visited a friend across in Sweden, at Lund, and she very kindly arranged for me to visit the Department of Obstetrics and Gynaecology at the medical school there. I was shown round by a gynaecologist and had some difficulty in explaining what was my particular interest, not because of any language difficulty—because, of course, his English was perfect—but because he considered family planning was so much a part of gynaecology that he could not think of it as a tiny speciality on its own.

Obstetricians and gynaecologists see women when their motivation is highest, namely, after childbirth or miscarriage. Furthermore, the two most popular methods of contraception, the contraceptive pill and I.U.D., come within the province of the gynaecologists and I shall return to this in a minute.

The third group of potential counsellors are the local health authority staff, and I am including the staff of the Family Planning Association clinic here because in many cases now, and increasingly in the future, the Family Planning Association clinics are on local authority premises and are held in collaboration with the local health authority. We have heard already and we are all agreed that family planning is an important part of preventive medicine and should have an assured place in the public health services. Midwives and health visitors have as close a view of family life as general practitioners and as great an opportunity for counselling.

The next question really arises out of the last: Where should family planning advice be given? Well, briefly, wherever it is asked for. That means in the doctor's surgery, in the local authority clinic, and, probably best of all, in the new health centres as they develop and as liaison also develops between the group practice and the local health authority, and in the hospitals. I want to stress this last point because it is in danger of being lost sight of although it has been mentioned by every speaker today. Both the English Act and the Northern Ireland circular specifically mention the powers of the local authority in providing family planning services. But they do not say that hospital authorities may not do so and I should be very sorry to see this interpretation put on the Ministry's circular here for three reasons.

In the first place, every lying-in hospital contains a very briefly captive population of highly motivated women, a few of whom may never be seen again till their next confinement. They already know the hospital staff and may be prepared to talk on this subject with them when they would not follow up referral to new contacts. Secondly, as I mentioned previously, the two most popular methods of contraception now are the contraceptive pill and I.U.D. Both are fringe benefits of gynaecology and should maintain some sort of connexion with hospital consultants. I myself feel fairly strongly that I.U.D.s are better inserted within a gynaecological department though I know that not everyone would agree with me. I am glad to see, incidentally, that this whole subject is recognized by the Royal College of Obstetricians and Gynaecologists who are now including family planning in their Diploma in Obstetrics. Finally, and very important, it is mainly in hospitals that students are trained, and if we want to produce doctors and nurses who have some knowledge of family planning then we must provide them with the clinical material—even though that is a horrible way to refer to patients. When should family planning advice be given? Well, of course, whenever it is asked for, and I would stress here that I do not think it is for a counsellor to judge a couple's decisions about this, but I do not think we should necessarily wait to be asked. I think family planning advice should be offered whenever it appears to be needed, and in particular postnatally and post-abortion. The need is something that should be looked for, and hospital and local authority clinics can arrange group talks in what the Americans, who always have a phrase for everything, call 'patient orientation'. I was doing it for sometime before I knew what I was up to! I think the gynaecologists should broach the subject with those sad ladies who trail their backaches and discharges and irregular bleedings round the out-patients' departments. Perhaps there should be some rule that when the outpatient's dossier reaches a certain weight nothing more should be done till family planning, in its broadest sense, has been fairly fully discussed. I was interested to hear from a general practitioner in Belfast that his prescriptions for tranquillizers have decreased as his pill prescriptions increased. And there is a general practitioner in Northampton who found that if he took time over family planning counselling interviews, his patients' subsequent attendances at the surgery decreased considerably.

The last question to be answered about counselling is, to whom should it be given? I think, broadly, to everyone who asks for it, because whoever asks for it must surely be in need. I do not want to labour the question of advice to the unmarried because it was gone into very fully this morning. I feel that at present in Ulster neither the local health authority nor the Family Planning Association are the right people to provide this service, though they may be in the future. The Family Planning Association is often asked about this and we say that our policy is to give advice to those who are married and those who are about to marry. But speaking now as an individual and not as a sort of official voice for the Family Planning Association, I do think we should be thinking of this and we have discussed the subject very fully this morning. I do not, however, want to overshadow the need for family planning for the married because this is a great need at present and there is not a sufficient opportunity for it in Ulster at the moment.

Nevertheless, I think that if the unmarried ask for advice then they should get it from someone, and if we are conferring on family planning for Ulster, we should think of this and of the need for something like the Brook clinics in England. In 1966 in Northern Ireland there were 1028 illegitimate births: 3 in 1000. We do not have a record here of pregnant brides, but everyone here must know of examples of this and pregnancy is not the best start to a marriage. There are obviously more causes of illegitimacy than lack of contraception, but advice in this is one approach to this problem.

I want now to turn to the second half of my title, techniques and materials available, which I am taking to cover broadly the whole subject of methods. I do not want to go into this in tremendous detail because many people here know a lot about it, but I want to mention some aspects of it.

Someone has said that the perfect contraceptive is 100 per cent effective, has no side-effects, does not interfere with spontaneity in intercourse, is easily reversible, and has no effect on subsequent fertility—and, of course, it does not exist. So the first thing to say about methods is that the counsellor and the patient between them must assess which of these factors matters most in this particular situation. In other words, the acceptability of the method is what matters most, and I include the medical acceptability to the doctor in that expression. I should like to stress again that the doctor must try to keep his own feelings out of this, or at least be aware of them. I find more and more that our patients expect 100 per cent effectiveness and they expect us to produce the ideal contraceptive, which is a thing we cannot do. One of the things that the family planning counsellor has to do is try to get over to the patient that life is not 100 per cent perfect and that we have to accept some of the imperfections of life.

In talking about family planning in Ulster there is another subject that I want to mention. At least one-third of our population are Roman Catholics. Catholics are not against family planning, and this is the first thing that non-Catholics ought to be clear about. Contrary to some people's beliefs they are in favour of it, but the only generally permitted method is the safe period, although everyone must be aware there is considerable debate within the Church about this. Anyone counselling in family planning in the North of Ireland must be able to instruct with conviction about how to use the safe period and this takes a lot of time at the beginning. This is something we should all understand and be able to help our patients about. However many arguments an individual doctor or nurse may be able to marshal against the method of the safe period—and we can all do this—if the couple want to use it then we must help them to use it, because it is the acceptable method for them.

In addition to this, everyone must have Catholic patients who have decided to use another method and are troubled and confused because of the apparent clash between their own consciences and the teaching of the Church. These people in particular need the caring and listening attitude of the counsellor to which I have already referred. They do not need advice; they need to be listened to. They must make up their own minds on this for each person's conscience is his or her own affair, but I am sure it helps to listen to difficulties.

The other aspect of this subject is that I have often felt in the past that apparent respect for Catholic feelings has been used as an excuse for some foot-dragging in respect of support for family planning. I have been told, for instance: 'We absolutely agree with your point of view but we do not want to offend anyone.' I think this is dishonest. If family planning is important it should be encouraged and a dialogue started between the two different points of view, and some arrangement made which, as far as possible, does not offend anyone's conscience. We are far too ready to assume attitudes without sufficient discussion, and this, of course, goes for many other situations besides Catholic and Protestant attitudes to family planning. But that is another lecture!

I do not want to say much more about methods. Many of the health visitors and midwives in the county health districts of Northern Ireland have already seen a very good film on techniques of contraception, and if any present have not seen it we will be glad to bring it round again. This film describes very fully the different methods, how they work, the advantages and disadvantages, the side-effects, and so on, but if any in the audience want to ask questions about these subjects I am sure the panel will be only too glad to answer them.

The only two methods I should like to say anything further about are oral contraceptives and sterilization, because of the counselling aspect of these. There has been so much publicity about the pill that patients can be very troubled about it. They know it is a very effective method, but they or their husbands have fears about the side-effects and they want to be able to discuss this. They are troubled in particular about the thrombo-embolism and possible carcinogenic effects. They may not ask about these, but they must be given the opportunity to ask.

It is, I think, important to take a good deal of time over the initial interview before putting a patient on the pill. I have had patients come to me and say: 'I want to use the pill but when I asked my doctor for it he said he didn't really approve of it and then gave me a prescription for 6 months' supply.' I think that is very unfair to the patient, the doctor, and the pill. The doctor should take great care in his first interview with a patient over the pill, explaining how it works and he should not stress too much the side-effects. Many people do not have any side-effects, but if a doctor starts suggesting them they will look for them. Leave it to the patient to get in touch if she is in any way worried. See her fairly often, which will give her a good start on the pill. Then there is the question of which pill to use. There used to be only three or four preparations; now there are many more and there is a wide choice. It is, I think, best to become familiar with a few, say from each main group, and restrict prescribing to these.

With regard to sterilization, Dr. Ramage has dealt fairly fully with the subject in the male, but I should like to say a few things about sterilization in women. Because of its irreversibility couples need plenty of time for reflection and discussion and this should, if possible, be done with both partners though this is not very often the case. I talk to a lot of women on this subject and they say: 'He leaves it to me.' I am not sure that that is very fair of 'him'. I think this is a decision they should take together, but, in fact, very often you will find that the husband is not brought into the discussion and just signs the consent form.

Then I also find that many women do not know, after the operation, what has happened to them. I have seen some patients who are surprised that they go on menstruating. A lot of time should be taken to explain what to expect. This is one of the fields of medicine where neighbours can be an awful pest and they can upset the whole business. I had a patient once and I thought that I had dealt with her problems about the pill for I had taken a good deal of time over her. She came back some time later and she told me she had stopped taking the pill because a woman at the bus stop, whom she had never met before, had told her that the pill was dangerous. We are up against a lot of folklore in this sphere of life.

With regard to sterilization, the neighbours always seem to know some-one who has had a pregnancy after the operation. Whether they all know the same neighbour I do not know, but, of course, it is a very reliable

5

operation. Another thing they are told about sterilization is that it only lasts for 7 years. I cannot trace the origin of this and if anyone here knows, I should love to discover it. This false information crops up all over the place, and it is worth going into it with the patient at the very start. You can say, 'Someone will tell you this, that, and the other thing but don't you listen to them', because they worry about it and they come back later worried about the whole business. Then they need to think about it not only from the point of view of the mechanics of the operation, but also from the sort of effect it is going to have on their feelings. In this regard they worry about intercourse. Most people, if anything, find that the enjoyment of intercourse increases, but if it was already poor and they are already frigid it is not going to improve that side of life.

They have to think about not being able to have any more babies. Women vary very much in their attitude to this subject of fertility. Some people feel a loss of femininity through their loss of fertility even though they do not want any more children; and at the other end of the scale are to be found women who cannot lose their breeding capacity quickly enough. You have to try to find out which sort of woman you are dealing with.

Finally, we come back to the individual's feeling about family planning, about family life, about children, and about a couple's feelings for one another. When we have said all we can about family planning as a public health service, and a necessity from the point of view of population control, the question of helping problem families, and its financial aspects, we come back in the end to the uniqueness and importance of each person. We return to what has already been said, that the real aims of family planning are quite positive, that couples should be helped to have the family that they want, and that each child that comes into the world arrives in a situation where it is loved and wanted and has the opportunities to realize its potential to the full.

THE CHAIRMAN: Thank you, Dr. Neill, for what I think everyone will agree is a very sensitive and very human approach to this problem of family planning with the emphasis on the individual and especially the woman concerned. It will be of great assistance to us as we look at the problems which arise.

Now, ladies and gentlemen, our final speaker is Dr. Aviva Wiseman. She comes to us from an area of Britain where family planning has been accepted for many years now. I would say that her district of Britain has led the field in many ways in regard to family planning. Her clinics are well known; she comes from Slough and is rather a 'peculiar' phenomenon in the family planning service in that she is an 'independent'. Dr. Wiseman has had wide experience over the past 10 years. She is concerned with the organization and administration of these clinics in the Slough area and these have now extended into other districts in Maidenhead and elsewhere. We are looking forward to her comments on this problem.

THE MUNICIPAL FAMILY PLANNING CLINIC IN ACTION

Dr. A. Wiseman

MR. CHAIRMAN, ladies, and gentlemen: As I have listened throughout the day to the other papers I have seen many of my own points whittled away by other people, so it may seem that my paper in places is rather a repetition of what has already been said. But that is one of the penalties of being the last speaker in a Conference such as this.

To many people a family planning clinic is simply a place where women can go to receive advice and supplies of some form of contraceptive method. Unhappily this has been true of many birth-control clinics in the past and still is true of some. But a much wider spectrum of interest must be covered if the family planning clinic is to play some part in counteracting the individual, community, and national problems which stem largely from the high rate of population growth. A close co-operation established between the services available at the clinics and those available in other departments under local authority auspices will help very much to further these aims.

Fundamentally a clinic must be concerned with birth-control methods, both conventional and the new pill and I.U.D., with additional sessions for investigation of sub-fertility, and cytology sessions where cervical smears can be taken for women who do not wish for other advice. The basic aim of the clinic must be to provide the best possible service within the field of family planning, and in congenial surroundings, where the attitude of the lay staff and the clinical approach of the medical and nursing staff will appeal to the greatest number of women of all social groups, which will bring them initially to the clinic for advice and induce their regular return for further visits.

The ideal situation for such a clinic is within a municipal health centre, where adjacent clinics of an advisory nature make referrals and discussions simple, where permanent premises could be available and the clinic office open daily for inquiries. Where no health centre is available the use of hospital premises is greatly to be desired, for it offers rooms already fitted as consulting and examination rooms. Both health centre and hospital premises commend themselves to patients as being buildings already familiar, easy of access, and having an aura of respectability to counteract the prejudice still prevailing in some areas which declares family planning to be not quite 'nice' and a matter to be discussed behind closed doors and in whispers.

How can we overcome the prejudices which still exist for many individuals in some social and religious groups and in certain communities? How can we help men and women to resolve the conflict between conscience, on the one hand, backed by generations of teaching that the natural function of man is procreation, and common sense, on the other, with the desire to provide fully in love, care, and education for the family they feel able to support? It is only by appreciating the many varied pressures on men and women in the matter of contraception, and attempting from the outset to counteract and prevail against them, that we can hope to set up the clinics which by their nature will attract women in the first instance and induce their regular further attendance.

The first visit of a woman to a family planning clinic is a great ordeal. She is about to discuss with complete strangers this most intimate aspect of her life. To many women menstrual and reproductive cycles are an entire mystery, shrouded in mists, superstitions, and ignorance with occasional more realistic descriptions gleaned only from the contorted tales passed on in school cloakrooms, or later by equally uninformed workmates. Some women are more knowledgeable, more worldly wise, but a certain embarrassment and shyness accompany every woman seeking contraceptive advice for the first time, and these mingle with fears aroused by old-wives' tales and superstitions and the inevitable long-distance stories of a friend of a friend of a friend, and her experience of contraception.

From such tales the new patient often has an accumulated wealth of misinformation regarding the procedures of interviewing, medical examination, and teaching of the method chosen, and it is vitally important to correct any misapprehension about the immediate and future visits to the clinic, about the various methods available, and the possible side-effects which each might or might not produce. Embroidered stories of contraceptive discomforts, side-effects, and failures circulate rather like the fabulous horror stories with which most young women are regaled during their first pregnancy, and these must be firmly and tactfully repudiated before prescribing any contraceptive method for any woman. As I have already remarked, much of this has already been touched on by previous speakers, and it is now only a matter of filling the gaps.

There are two points I should like to mention here. Firstly, no new patient should ever be turned away, however busy the clinic may be. This may result in occasional protracted sessions for the staff, but the important person is the patient, and she may have been considering a visit for some time and finally screwed up her courage to come along. To send her away now or ask her to make a further appointment may discourage her completely from further attendance. So often this is a woman who needs help and advice very urgently and it is particularly important that she be seen by the doctor this first time that she has visited a family planning clinic.

Secondly, every new patient must see the doctor. No personal prejudices or opinions shall decide that an individual woman should not be attending a clinic. This relates particularly to the unmarried, some of whom inform the interviewer that they do not intend to marry for some time but are seeking contraceptive advice. I know that there are some people who feel strongly that these girls should not attend family planning clinics, or indeed be given any contraceptive advice, and if it is to be done it should be done at special clinics such as the Brook clinics. But they should be interviewed and come through to the doctor with no comment, no special folder, no discrimination. It is then the responsibility of the doctor to listen to the girl's reason for coming, to offer advice and guidance, and discuss the problems and hazards that lie ahead.

If the girl, or woman, remains determined to continue her liaison or embark upon a sex relationship, then it is unwise and medically unsound to withhold the prescribing of a contraceptive method. I do not believe that we are causing these young people to become promiscuous. Some of them already are promiscuous and must be safeguarded from the results of their own behaviour. Others for reasons which seem good and sincere to them have a steady relationship. Either girl is going to be at risk of pregnancy, and if she becomes pregnant she may seek abortion and suffer all the physical and emotional trauma which that entails, or if she decides to have her baby then she must undergo the difficulties and hardships of the unmarried mother. Whatever the outcome it will almost inevitably lead to a call on local authority resources and finances.

As the Chairman has told you, I am associated with the clinic in Slough. It is an independent, charitable organization which is run on its own but in which we are fortunate to have very close co-operation from the local health authority and the members of the staff. I want now to say something about how these clinics are run. The administration is carried out by a committee representing medical, nursing and lay staff of the clinics and representatives of the medical officer of health's office, midwives, general practitioners, and consultant gynaecologists. In this way all sections of opinion can be aired and shared, and the clinic run with continuing close liaison between the different departments within the clinic and the interested groups outside it, with a close relationship of purpose between them all.

The staff are paid on a sessional basis, and all staff should be paid, including the lay workers, so establishing a really high level of efficiency. We have no voluntary workers except one, who has been with the clinic since it began. We feel that we cannot get a really high level of efficiency with voluntary workers.

Fees and charges to women attending should be kept as low as is compatible with outgoings and overheads, but most women can pay the fees at present in effect in Family Planning clinics. Most prefer to pay for what is, to them, an important and worth-while service. Some cannot afford to pay the full rate but prefer to pay something, even if it is on an instalment basis. For those who truly cannot afford anything we must be prepared to supply them free of charge. Medical cases are already indicated for free supplies, but equally important are the social cases which will become medical problems unless something is done. To determine these we must rely largely on the health visitor who knows her families and who knows which women should, for social or domestic reasons, be helped to avoid a further pregnancy.

Sometimes a woman is unwilling or unable to visit a clinic, but would be willing to discuss contraception with a Family Planning doctor in her own home. This domiciliary service is essential as an approach to the hard core of women who most urgently need help. The consent of the general practitioner is, of course, essential to this initial home visiting.

In Southampton, where Dr. Dorothy Morgan has pioneered this work, it has been so well accepted that the local authority now sponsors and finances it. The saving in time and money which would have been spent on maternity benefits, child care, hospital treatment, and the myriad demands of further unwanted children born into what are often already problem families is very great. This work is being carried out in other parts of England, and reports of its value in terms of improved health and family conditions are most encouraging for the many who engage in this difficult, often unsalubrious, and time-consuming work. Many visits must often be paid before the confidence of the woman is gained, and she and her husband become convinced that contraception has merit for them. These women are often of low intelligence and lack motivation. For so many of them repeated pregnancy is an accepted event. It is the one achievement in which they can find fulfilment. They are aware of no other desires or ambitions, for life and education have shown them no alternative.

So it is often a long and tedious job to make them understand and appreciate the advantages of family planning for them. Once they have understood this and have started an acceptable method of contraception, a high percentage of women remain faithful users. The failure rate, though greater than amongst women of higher intelligence and greater motivation, is not untoward and when there is an unplanned pregnancy the woman, in almost every case, resumes contraceptive practice after delivery.

It is interesting also that many of these women gain in self-confidence and self-respect when established on an effective contraceptive method, and will come to the clinic within the first year for an examination and the very important cervical smear, and often continue to visit in order to collect further supplies.

Ideally a clinic would be open 5 days a week so that a woman can come at any time and be seen or at least find an office open for inquiries. An evening clinic is essential in most areas, for some women work or cannot leave their families in the day time, and it is important to make it easy for them to make their visits.

Each of our sessions is officially 1–1½ hours long—this is for admission of patients—but actual working time will, of course, be at least twice this length, to allow for the setting up of the clinic and for the interviewing, consultation, and teaching of patients already waiting.

A working unit at a session comprises one doctor, one nursing sister, and one lay worker, although in the event of a clinic with only one doctor, two lay workers are needed, one for reception and one for dispensing. Where the attendance warrants it, sessions of two or three doctors working together have very great advantages, for more time can be given to individual patients where necessary, without producing a complete block for others waiting. This ability to spend time and give relaxed attention is of immense importance in matters connected with family planning. An average of 20 patients can then be seen in a session, even though an occasional individual may need 20–30 minutes.

As regards appointments for the general clinics, it is difficult to operate a fixed appointment system, where time per patient varies, and domestic situations or illness in her family can easily cause alterations or delays. Simple but perfectly satisfactory is an approximation whereby further attendances are booked for a specific date but not time; and women are requested to come on that date but assured that if they are, for personal reasons, unable to keep that appointment they will be seen at an earlier or later date as it suits them. I realize that this may seem to be spoon-feeding our clientele, but the patient is the important person. Not many take advantage of such a system. The majority will keep regular appointments and make great efforts to do so, but an absolute unchangeable appointments system deters some women, and keeps away those who should come for advice or reassurance earlier than their next fixed visit.

What is going to bring women to the clinic in the first instance and, having made an initial visit, what will keep them attending regularly? A certain number come because they have talked to friends or relatives already attending. This personal link is the best recommendation. Some few have read about family planning clinics and will go to the trouble of looking up phone numbers and addresses. An increasing number come having been advised to do so by their own doctor, by the midwife, or by the health visitor. It is the co-operation of the midwife and the health visitor in particular which determines whether a clinic is to reach the women in most urgent need of help.

Additionally in some areas doctors from family planning clinics are invited to maternity wards to discuss family planning and contraceptive methods with new mothers, and many midwives are starting discussion on the subject at antenatal classes and clinics. These various means will introduce the idea to would-be users of a contraceptive method and should be extended, but the clinic must produce the right atmosphere and a widely acceptable 'image'.

Every patient must be made to feel welcome and treated at each encounter with different members of the staff as an individual, not as a cipher. She should know that during each interview her welfare is the sole and personal interest of the member of staff to whom she is speaking. Privacy is essential, and time is necessary, especially at the first visit.

All patients are weighed at every visit and blood-pressure is taken at initial and yearly visits, unless a high reading is found at the start or in a woman with a history of toxaemia, when more frequent readings are necessary. Family planning clinics are a brand of 'well woman' clinics where a great deal of information is amassed. It is worth considering the central recording of information available to determine possible effects of forms of contraception, and to elicit facts regarding the general health of women of the reproductive age-group.

Most women come to the clinic having decided on their chosen method, but time given to discussion and elimination of any doubts or mistaken ideas is well spent at this stage, whatever the method. In our experience the majority of women who come for the pill can often be seen by the doctor in groups of three or more for a general discussion on the mode of action of the pill, and points of interest in connexion with this. Then it is only a matter of moments to examine and take a cervical smear as necessary and prescribe. Cap patients, of course, must be seen individually, and it is advisable that I.U.D. patients be seen at a special session, where perhaps a firmer appointment system can be operated.

I could go on talking for a long time about the first visit to the clinic because it is this first discussion between doctor and patient which will set the whole pattern for her in regard to her acceptance of the method of contraception and it will reflect, too, on her general well-being. Therefore, I consider it very important that this interview should be as long and detailed as is necessary to reassure the patient and answer her spoken and unspoken queries.

The doctor must write the prescription and give the date of the next appointment. Cap patients are seen a week after the initial visit, then at intervals of 3 or 6 months. Pill users return after 6 weeks, then at 3-monthly intervals, but when they are happily established on a pill régime they need only be seen by the doctor at 6-monthly intervals, returning to collect further tablets at the intervening 3-monthly visit. I.U.D. users return about 6 weeks after insertion of the device and then for yearly checks. With all these users there is always the understanding, repeated to them frequently, that they may return at any clinic, or telephone the doctor if they are worried in any way.

The family planning doctor must be a specialist in family planning. For this training sessions are needed where the interested doctor can learn about all methods of contraception—their relative advantages and disadvantages, and indications for and against different methods. She must have opportunities for practical experience of the prescribing, teaching, fitting, and management of the various methods, so that these sessions are best held within the framework of a busy clinic, where teaching and practice can be combined.

The family planning doctor must be sympathetic and understanding of the particular reticence and shyness of the premarital girl and the general problems—marital, domestic, sexual as well as medical—of the married woman and the additional problems of the premenopausal woman. Caring for and advising these women is well within the scope of an experienced trained family planning doctor, who needs no additional psychiatric training nor further gynaecological degrees to deal with the majority of the problems which come her way, knowing always that if the problems are too great they can be referred to the specialist concerned.

I suppose you have noticed that I keep using the word 'she' when referring to the family planning doctor. That is the position in most of our clinics, for the women who come to them prefer to see a lady doctor. They say they cannot discuss such personal matters with their own general practitioner. On the other side of the issue is the fact that family planning work is an excellent opening for a married woman doctor who prefers to go out for only fixed sessions. The experience of her own pregnancy and her own married life will enable her to bring her own common sense to bear on the problems placed before her and that is really all that is required in dealing with many of the problems that come her way.

Another aspect of family planning is the opportunity it affords to participate in preventive medicine. Women visiting clinics frequently have medical and personal problems which they are unable to discuss in the first instance with their own doctor, or admit to an unwillingness to intrude on a doctor's busy surgery to ask about something which may turn out to be unimportant and require only reassurance but no treatment. Such a patient finds it easier to talk to the clinic doctor because this doctor is also a woman, and many women confess themselves unable to broach the subject of such things as vaginal discharges, breast discomfort, or fear of a lump with their own general practitioner. However, having discussed it and with the subject mentioned in an accompanying letter from the clinic, she will go to her own doctor for the advice and treatment which she needs. The clinic doctor may equally discover on inquiry or examination conditions which need treatment, particularly now that with the increased use of cervical smears vaginal infections are being identified, and the patient is referred back to her own general practitioner with a letter regarding the findings and a copy of the smear report where applicable for treatment or further referral.

The great importance for the welfare of the patient is the mutual understanding and regard between clinic doctor and general practitioner. In an area where the clinic is run on ethical lines, the general practitioners will come to respect the purpose of the clinic doctors, to know that their patients are in good hands, and to realize that letters requesting treatment or referral are designed to help the general practitioner, to save his or her time, and deserve immediate action. In a similar way close liaison with the gynaecologist is important, not only in the matter of referring patients for treatment, but in being kept informed of the progress of the patients and co-operation in the follow-up. The family planning clinic, with its allied services in cytology particularly, can and must play an important part in preventive medicine, and, when utilized to the full and in co-operation with present welfare services, can help to produce a happier, healthier community. On the financial side, although this will call for outlay at the start in setting up the clinics and financing needy cases, the long-term accounting over all welfare services has been shown in many areas, already operating similar schemes, to be advantageous.

To sum up, municipal family planning clinics should be set up to cater for the needs of women of all social groups, of all educational levels, of differing financial status, of all races and language, and of all religious persuasions. In this context it would be well to consider ways and means of filling the gaps in the knowledge of young and older people, and trying to prevent the absorption and accumulation of mistaken ideas, by giving talks and having discussions on human anatomy, physiology, and sex relationships, family planning and contraception. These can take place on clinic premises. Simple visual aids and films can be used.

The lecturers and teachers must be carefully chosen, not only for their specialized knowledge, but also for their understanding and deep concern for the welfare and well-being of the community at large. These are subjects which can easily produce embarrassment when taught by the wrong people, and the advantages of the information gained are cancelled out by the tensions generated. So often unhappily this is the case in schools when a member of staff is designated to give the talk on sex education simply because he or she happens to have a free period at the right time, and for no other reason. We must strive to educate men, women, and children in these matters in the hope that the new generation of patients will be able to inform their own children directly and in a knowledgeable way, so allowing them to grow up with an awareness of the implications of sex, its emotional as well as its physical effects, and thereby decrease the pitfalls which beset the completely ignorant.

With these particular aspects being dealt with in co-operation with the education department, with cytology clinics available for women desiring a smear only, with pregnancy tests performed as necessary on the premises, with special sessions for the investigation of infertility, and the main sessions for family planning advice, the municipal clinic can offer a truly comprehensive service to the women who attend.

THE CHAIRMAN: Dr. Wiseman, we have had to wait right to the end of the Conference for your contribution, but I am sure, ladies and gentlemen, you would agree with me that it has been well worth waiting for. This paper is packed full with practical and valuable information for all who are engaged in the day-to-day running of family planning clinics. I hope we will have an opportunity to read this paper in detail at a later time.

DISCUSSION AT AFTERNOON SESSION

DR. J. LOUGHRAN: I am one of those rather odd bods from down south with weird ideas on the morality of family planning. Strangely enough the wind of change has actually blown south of the border in Ireland. I hope, seriously, that very much benefit will come to us from this most interesting symposium today, and I should like very much to thank the organizers, Ortho Pharmaceutical Limited, and the medical staff for what I regard as remarkable lectures. 'The pill' is being used on a wide scale, and we find, in a community where there are not the lines of communication to publicize it and the full facts concerning it, that there is most disquieting misinformation about its safety.

The question I should like to ask our expert panel is the relative risk to the woman using the pill compared with, for example, the woman using the rhythmic method. I should also like to put another question which arises from a survey published in the *British Medical Journal* of 27 April, 1968, from which it appears that the mortality risk from the use of the pill is about one-fifteenth of all the pregnancies, that is for the year. Would the panel not agree that a failure rate of more than ten-fifteenths, or 7 per cent, represents a greater risk to women and would they know of any device with a lower failure rate? I can only think of one, the I.U.D. device, and as a supplementary question may I ask, based on its failure rate of 2–3 per cent, whether the panel would not agree that one can theoretically regard the I.U.D. device as one of the safest methods of family planning, or does it also have a predictable mortality of its own?

PROFESSOR PINKERTON: Dr. Loughran has asked and answered his question at the same time. I can see nothing wrong with his arithmetic, but then I am not a mathematician. The important point of the survey that was made is that we are not comparing the effect on women of the pill against the population of women who are just not taking the pill, but against the population of women who if they do not do something will be pregnant. It is extraordinary how often this obvious fact is lost sight of in a discussion of this sort.

As to the I.U.C.D., there has been a delightful word 'translocation' coined for when it penetrates the wall of the uterus; my impression is that this accident is not as common here as in Singapore. Whether that is because we do not use so many here or because we do it better I do not know.

DR. J. G. NEILL: I am not much good at mental arithmetic but Dr. Loughran's statistics sound fine to me as far as I can take them in. According to them it seems that I.U.D. is the safest device, but it has disadvantages, in particular the question of excessive bleeding. Something like 10 per cent have to be removed because of this. A proportion of women find it unacceptable; they do not like the idea of a foreign body in the uterus. We come back to the idea that you have to choose what suits the patient. I am sure this is really the answer to what contraceptive to use and because patients are different the answer is different.

DR. G. RAMAGE: We all know that there is very little that we do in this life to which there is no risk attached. We have to take some risks and all we can do is take the minimum. I think it is entirely wrong to suggest to any woman that these methods are entirely without risk. We should adopt a common-sense approach to this problem as well.

DR. A. WISEMAN: This question of risk is something to put into perspective, for our patients and the figures from the Dunlop Committee make it apparent that there are some side-effects on the pill. In any case the risk of taking the pill is considerably less than the risk we take every day in crossing the road. You must try to put it into everyday terms; that is what I try to do when I am asked about this.

DR. W. EDGAR: One of the many advantages of the pill is that it keeps the women younger than they would otherwise be. I know of no statistics on this point. I was once asked to speak to a men's club about cancer on the lung and I gave them the sort of statistical information that is available. A member of the audience said, 'I understand that a very heavy cigarette smoker has a one in eight chance of dying from this disease. Does this mean you have a seven in eight chance of *not* dying from it?' It depends on how you wish to interpret statistical information!

DR. R. CARSON: I am the Medical Officer of Health in Limavady, Co. Londonderry, and get quite a lot of mothers, especially Service mothers, and they like to come back to Ireland. When they go away they get the pill posted to them and when they return—I have been there 10 years—they ask me about any long-term side-effects. I have to hedge because I know myself there are some sorts of side-effects. But are there any long-term side-effects from the pill for those continuously or intermittently on the pill for 2, 3, or 5 years? I do not honestly know, but perhaps the panel we have here today should enlighten me on that point.

DR. A. WISEMAN: I can only say that in Slough we have been using the pill since August, 1960, and so there are some women in Slough who have been on it continuously for 8 years. Occasionally we have to change the pill. I am not sure that this is truly a side-effect but rather that a woman, who having been 4 years on one particular pill, wants another of a different colour. There are hundreds of thousands of women who have been using the pill through clinics for 6 years and there are others who to my knowledge have been using it for 8 years and I cannot say that I have found any untoward effects.

The worrying thing for some women who are absolutely happy on the pill is in regard to the length of time she can stay on it. I have had patients say to me. 'I have been 2 years on the pill and I know I may not stay any longer than 2 years on it.' This started at the beginning of the trials, when we were told in England that a woman could only remain for 1 year on the pill. So we played that one by ear and before the year was up we found that in America there were those happily on it for 6 years. So the time in England was extended to 2 years, then 4 years, and now there is no limit, provided that the woman is fit and well and wishes to continue. This is all part of the folklore of this business. So far as I can judge there are few side-effects of any serious nature. Sometimes it is found that women are pushing their weight up and we try to get it down. The best way to do this is to tell them that unless they begin to lose weight within the next 3 months they will have to come off the pill. It is remarkable how quickly the weight will come down!

DR. R. CARSON: Are there any ill effects of the pill on a long-term basis? This is the sort of question that is thrown at me at family social groups and that sort of thing.

PROFESSOR PINKERTON: The short answer to that is, we do not know. There have certainly been no ill-effects demonstrated with the pill and it has been used now for many years; if any serious side-effects were going to develop we would have heard about them by now. They may develop in 40 years' time; I do not know; certainly there is no evidence that the pill is causing cancer of the endometrium, indeed the evidence points in the other direction. The other organ women sometimes worry about is the breast and whether oestrogen has the effect of inducing cancer of the breast. There is no doubt that some cancers of the breast are oestrogen sensitive, but by no means all; I know of no evidence that oestrogen *induces* the growth of breast cancer in the human species. There is no evidence either that oestrogen will cause the growth of fibroids. I do not think there is any evidence whatsoever that neoplasm, either benign or malignant, has been induced by the use of progrestongen mixtures.

DR. HOPKINS: I am a general practitioner and I should like to ask a question about the I.U.D. device. How long does a woman have to wait for this to be carried out in Belfast? I understand there is a waiting list.

DR. J. G. NEILL: It depends on the woman. It is true we have a long waiting list. The fittings are done at the Royal Maternity and at Dundonald. We are hoping soon, too, to start at the City Hospital which I hope will relieve matters slightly. We do up to 20 a week at the Royal Maternity Hospital. There is a priority list.

DR. HOPKINS: I recently sent a letter to the Royal Maternity but I got no reply. I understood there was some screening going on.

DR. J. G. NEILL: The situation is that if any person does not qualify to be seen at the Royal Maternity she should go to one of the other family planning clinics. The object of screening is to see that the persons applying are suitable.

Dr. Hopkins: The difficulty is that the people I have in mind are in West Belfast and Dundonald is too far away for them. I have a particular person in mind and she was to go on the waiting list. She had already used a diaphragm which she found unsatisfactory. I put her on the pill but she now has to come off the pill.

Dr. J. G. Neill: If you give me her name we will see what can be done.

Mrs. Chalkley: I am Chairman of the Federation of Women's Guilds, I am already a woman's counsellor, and I have done education work with the Marriage Guidance Council. Much has been said about promiscuity and helping the young unmarried couple as well as lectures in schools. The point to make here is that very few people in schools realize that in the 15–16 age-groups there are those who could be married at that time. I should like to ask a question about the premenopausal woman. Apart from what Dr. Wiseman said about her special needs, is it not a fact that there is little special help in the way of family planning advice for such women?

Dr. A. Wiseman: This is a terribly important question. We do see a lot of women who come to the clinic at this particular time in their lives. They have fears about the possibility of a pregnancy at a time when they are already grandmothers and as well they may have anxieties about fibroids and cancer and other things. They are unhappy, and—I say this with the greatest respect—the general practitioners as a whole are unsympathetic listeners. So we are prepared to spend a lot of time talking to them. We give them a full and extensive examination, both breast and pelvic, and as far as we can, we find out by examination whether they are completely fit women who happen to be premenopausal and who want absolute protection from a late pregnancy. They want to give pleasure to their partners but they are afraid of the risk involved. These women want the pill and we give it to them where necessary. With the fear of pregnancy removed they are more relaxed, and they can go back to their husbands and once more become interested in the sexual intercourse which had become such a burden to them because of fear. At this stage of life they know that if they are unable to do this the husband will look elsewhere and there is the possibility of their marriage breaking up.

I was once accused of talking about giving people the pill and so interfering with the perfect clockwork mechanism of the female body and the menstrual cycle. My answer is that I do not believe any woman has a perfect menstrual cycle. It is almost inevitable that women have some sort of menstrual misery, brought on by irregular periods, heavy bleeding, and so on. There are so many things which can upset someone who is otherwise a perfectly normal woman. These things are increased and aggravated as one gets to the premenopausal stage. By putting such women on the pill not only does it help them sexually, but they become in a great many cases much fitter persons. They are much more relaxed and happier. An interesting thing is that we have reached the stage when some of the women on the pill are approaching the age when they wait for symptoms of the menopause to turn up which will tell them that they can come off the pill. But they find that they are not occurring and they ask us: 'How do we know when we are past the age for producing an infant and can stop being on the pill?' The answer to that is: 'We do not know.' This is because the average age of the menopause has gone up to about 48. Very many women in the fifties who are on the pill menstruate quite regularly. I am happy to keep them on the pill until we know the answer to this. Some say, 'At the age of 52 you should take them off the pill and find out!'

THE CHAIRMAN: In drawing this Family Planning for Ulster Conference to a close I should like, first of all, to thank you, our audience, for your kindness to us today and for paying such rapt attention to the papers which you have heard. It has been a long day but this has been a most excellent conference in my opinion. The speakers, who have spoken so often, are, I am sure, pleased with the response from the audience, especially this afternoon. By expressing yourselves freely we hope that you have been able to get answers to your questions. But for you and your participation a conference of this kind could not be a success. We thank you, ladies and gentlemen.

It now gives me great pleasure to thank our speakers for their contribution to our Conference today. It would be presumptuous of me—and I am sure you would not wish me to do it even if I could—to try in any way to sum up the papers that we have heard. All our speakers have been first class. Professor Pinkerton's contribution this morning mentioned the question of cost which was a very valid point. I hope his remarks will reach the proper quarter and that something quickly will follow to get some more money for our family planning work. We appreciate very much the contributions of those who came over from England to speak to us and we are grateful, too, to Mrs. Greeves, of the Marriage Guidance Council, for the most fascinating way she painted the picture of her organization, how it fits into the whole picture of family planning, and how all these services must come closer together and get to know each other. Dr. Joyce Neill is well known here and her contribution was in every way excellent. I would combine her with Dr. Wiseman, both of whom are working in the everyday world of family planning and whose advice to us and whose information are of vital importance to anyone who is undertaking this work. I hope we will have an opportunity to read these papers at some later time because they require some study.

DR. G. RAMAGE: This is my first visit to Ireland and so I am different from Dr. Edgar who was on his honeymoon here. It is a little late for me to have a honeymoon, but nevertheless Dr. Edgar could not have been happier that I have been on this visit. To come here and participate in a programme on this most important subject in public health and indeed for the community; to come here and myself benefit from hearing my colleagues speak; to come here and see such a large audience, all this has been a very happy occasion for me and I think I am right in the feeling that everybody here has enjoyed today. This would have been impossible had it not been for the public-spirited and disinterested action of Ortho Pharmaceutical Limited who have made this possible.

When I was asked to participate I was asked if I would speak on a certain subject. I was not asked to say what I was going to say and I had not any exact knowledge of what my colleagues were going to say. It was completely open and independent and that is the way such a conference as this should be. I only hope we have not in any way exceeded the bounds that our organizers intended.

I look upon it as a privilege to finish this evening in expressing my own personal thanks as well as the warmest thanks of us all for this public-spirited attitude by Ortho Pharmaceutical Limited in organizing this Conference and sending Mr. George in person, a man who has given us much helpful assistance.